home cooking

a recipe collection

home cooking
around the **world**

david ricketts

photographs by mark thomas

stewart, tabori & chang | *new york*

APR 2002

Published in 2001 by

Stewart, Tabori & Chang

A company of La Martinière Groupe

115 West 18th Street

New York, NY 10011

Library of Congress Cataloging-in-Publication Data

Ricketts, David.

   Homecooking around the world : a recipe collection / David Ricketts ; photographs by Mark Thomas.

     p. cm.

   ISBN 1-58479-092-X

     1. Cookery, International. I. Title.

TX725.A1 R534 2001

641.59—dc21   2001031469

Printed in Singapore

10 9 8 7 6 5 4 3 2 1

First Printing

for arthur and gertrude,

my eighty-something parents,

who continue to search

for the perfect lobster roll

contents

seafood

vegetables

desserts

I loved to eat as a kid—and guess what? I still do. I grew up with home cooking—and that kind of cooking is the focus of this book, whether it's supper in Hanoi, Lima, Ubud, Bangkok, Deer Isle, Wellfleet, or

home cooking— where does it begin?

New York City, and whether it's in a home kitchen or a mom-and-pop restaurant that serves home-style food. What I've learned about home cooking over the years, both from my professional food career and from traveling, is that the main ingredients are usually very similar, regardless of where you are. It's the seasonings that make the difference. So in one respect, this book is really an exploration of the wonderful world of herbs and spices.

But let me begin at the beginning. I am of the generation, just post–World War II and pre–baby boom, for whom the kitchen—and on Sundays the dining room—was the center of home life. Television and computers had not yet intruded, so conversation—the precursor to Internet chat rooms—was one of our forms of amusement.

Dinner at our house, much as in the television sitcoms of the 1950s, was always at the prescribed hour of six o'clock. My father usually walked through the back door at around five-thirty, then changed and washed. When my Mom called out, "Dinner!" my brother and I dropped what we were doing and headed for the kitchen. We sat and ate for at least a half-hour, often longer, sharing our stories from the day.

My mother, as I learned many years later, never really liked to cook, but you wouldn't know it from the table she set. She made a lot of things from scratch, with little reliance on convenience foods. Her repertoire consisted of a broad range of dishes: beef stew, roasted leg of lamb, roasted chicken, Swiss steak, codfish cakes, spaghetti with homemade tomato sauce and meatballs, date-nut bread, cheesecake, fruit crumbles and cobblers, and on and on. She was always clipping recipes from the newspapers and magazines, and those that got more than just a silent response from the dinner table were added to her wooden recipe box.

Restaurant-going was always a major event for our family. We didn't do a lot of it, but when we did, I was so excited I could hardly eat. Since I grew up in Connecticut, close to New York City, we would drive into Manhattan every now and then for theater and dinner out, eating in such classic spots as Schrafft's, Horn & Hardart, and Lindy's, where the dishes we ordered were basically restaurant versions of what we ate at home.

Now fast-forward to the late 1960s: My first trip abroad, during an era when America's youth were experiencing their rites of passage on the roads and in the youth hostels and campgrounds of Europe. I joined them, riding a motorcycle, with no fear and the enthusiasm and never-satisfied curiosity of a twenty-one-year-old. Traveling with a friend, I saw most of Europe, including Yugoslavia and Czechoslovakia when those countries were still under Communist control. And I ate, and ate, and ate, and as a result, my vision of home cooking expanded exponentially. If I wasn't eating with families I had met on the road, then I was exploring small mom-and-pop restaurants that were really just extensions of the home kitchen. Food was the background against which I talked with people and learned about their lives and their cultures.

In the less touristy northern part of the Mediterranean island of Corfu, my friend and I stumbled upon an open pavilion on the beach, sheltering two picnic tables. A young man and woman with three kids were sitting and laughing on the beach near an open grill. It was around five in the afternoon. Covered with dirt, we parked our motorcycles—so *Easy Rider*—and headed for a glass case at one side of the pavilion. The young man waved and walked toward us, smiling. We didn't speak the language he spoke, and vice versa. Now that we were close enough, we could see that the case held three or four kinds of whole fish on ice. I pointed to a reddish fish, and then to

the grill out on the beach. The young man flashed me a big grin, gave me the thumbs-up sign, and then motioned to a tub of greens behind the case. I shook my head *yes*. After my friend made his choice, we sat down at a picnic table, and one of the kids brought over a chilled bottled of retsina and two glasses. The young man tossed a few fennel twigs on the coals and threw our fish on top. Soon the whole gang, laughing and shouting, brought our dinner to us on large white platters: the fish; a salad with the ripest tomatoes, drizzled with a green olive oil and red-wine vinegar; and a long loaf of bread with a crispy crust. The fish was subtly perfumed with the smoke from the fennel branches, and the flavors of the salad were simple and pure. This wasn't really a restaurant; this was home cooking at its most memorable. About an hour and a half later, two grinning, slightly tipsy American boys, after hugging their hosts good-bye, climbed back on their motorcycles. And so continued my love affair with life and simple home cooking.

Fast-forward another fifteen years. I was spending the Christmas holidays in Paris with a very close friend, and early one evening we were both craving choucroute, the classic Alsatian version of hot dogs with sauerkraut. We headed for the Brasserie Terminus-Nord near the Gare du Nord, where we were shown to a small table covered with crisp white linen in the center of the huge room. We wasted no time in placing our order. The choucroute arrived: several different kinds of sausage and smoked pork chops peeking out from mounds of caraway-scented sauerkraut. The jars of *moutarde* were already on the table. My hazy recollection is that we finished off two bottles of an Alsatian white wine that evening. Home cooking at its best, brasserie-style.

Fast-forward another fifteen years. This time the scene is Saigon, now known as Ho Chi Minh City. Some friends and I were in a tiny cab, heading for the Andong Market, housed in an imposing but drab four-story building in the Chinese district—the Cholon. What we were looking for was in the basement of that building: a hodge-podge collection of food stalls. We found them, and after crisscrossing the vast expanse several times, checking out cleanliness, friendliness of owners, and the selection of bubbling pots, we finally picked one where several people were already eating at small tables. We plunked our bags down on four stools and strolled over to the kitchen area, sniffing and taking a look at the simmering broths, the different types of noodles in separate bowls, and all the add-ins: chiles, green leafy herbs, pork ribs, mushrooms—the selection was endless. Then the fun started. We pointed at various pots and bowls and assembled our own Vietnamese smorgasbord. It was just another home-cooked meal, but this time with a lot of uninvited guests.

Here's my point: What we call "home cooking" can be found all over, even in the most unexpected places. Around the world, food is woven intimately into people's everyday activities, and the food on the streets is, more often than not, the same as at home. A Vietnamese worker will often start the day with a bowl of noodles in hot broth with slivers of meat. He may serve himself at home, dunking a

ladle into a pot on the kitchen stove, or he may assemble his bowl of steaming chicken noodle soup from a street vendor. In Lima, Peru, lunch could be a skewer of barbecued beef hearts, again purchased from a street vendor. What sets the United States apart from most other countries is the fact that we are a car culture. Except for perhaps New York City, there are very few places in the U.S. where you can walk to everything—and get a good meal at a street cart.

For the past twenty-five years, as I've worked editorially with food, I've stood back and taken note of how the home-eating habits in our country have changed. When I was fifteen years old, my mother would often spend half a day fixing dinner. Now for meals at home, a fifteen-minute prep time is often the norm—and many people don't even do that, opting instead for fast food at its worst: a meat patty served on a bun, with flavor and texture engineered for universal appeal, and passed into the front seat of a car from a window at a drive-through restaurant. Nothing has been left to chance in the creation of that product. I know—I've been part of professional focus groups that have shaped such products!

One of my intentions in this book is to look at home cooking in a variety of countries, and to see what recipes tell us about those cultures. For instance, in Southeast Asia, the absence of beef or its use only in small amounts in cooking may point to a lack of grazing land, which is actually the case since most of the land is devoted to rice production. In Bali, the fact that roasted suckling pig is virtually the national dish of this small island, one among thousands in the predominantly Muslim archipelago of Indonesia, might lead you to suspect that Bali is not Muslim. You would be right, since the majority of its residents are Hindu, a religion that has no proscription against eating pork. In Vietnam, beef stew with carrots reflects almost a thousand years of Chinese occupation and a hundred years of French colonialism: a small amount of meat in the stew reflects the Chinese influence, and the carrots the French. In the cooking of Kerala Province in southwest India, bordered by the Arabian Ocean, the use of coconut milk and shredded coconut is only natural, since there is an abundance of coconut palms. These palms thrive in the salty sea air and sandy soil. Hard to believe that a simple recipe can tell you all this.

As I've mentioned before, what generally distinguishes one cuisine from another are the taste and aroma of the food, as affected by herbs and spices and other seasoning elements. Consider the potato. Having originated in Peru, the potato was carried by the Spanish and Portuguese to Europe and other places. Although basically the same kind of potato is used around the world, with some variations, the preparation relies on available seasonings and the local palate. In Peru, for one popular dish called *Papas a la Huancaina,* the potatoes are boiled, sliced, and then blanketed with a chile-spiked cheese sauce, and garnished with corn, tomato, and hard-cooked eggs. The Swedish dish Jansson's Temptation features scalloped potatoes seasoned with fennel seeds and anchovies. Cape Cod Clam Pie is another potato-and-seafood combination, but flavored with aromatic vegetables, bacon, and thyme. Irish *Colcannon* is mashed potatoes mixed with leeks and cabbage or kale and a pinch of nutmeg. The Potato-and-Celery-Root Gratin with Prosciutto is yet another scalloped-potato dish with heavy cream, but accented with cheese and prosciutto. A potato is a potato is a potato, but what it tastes like when it arrives at the dinner table depends on who's cooking it. I could make the same case for the carrot, which shows up in dishes as varied as Vietnamese Spicy Beef Stew with Carrots and Star Anise, Chicken Pot Pie with Pecan–Sour Cream Pastry, and Flemish Carbonnade with Carrots.

Although at first glance my collection of recipes may seem to be randomly eclectic, there is an underlying set of criteria for each choice. I always have in mind, as a starting point, a basic recipe that is familiar to the American home cook. What is intriguing, I think, is to find the same dish prepared in another culture, with its different seasonings and other flavoring elements. For instance, chicken noodle soup becomes Vietnamese Chicken Noodle Soup with Fresh Herbs; beef stew, African Beef-and-Kale Stew with Pumpkin-Seed Sauce; beef Stroganoff, Indonesian Spicy Beef in Coconut Sauce; fish and chips, Balinese Fried Fish with *Sambal;* and a New England boiled dinner, South American Beef-and-Potato Stew with Peaches.

Part of my approach to food has always included the consideration of a recipe as more than just a set of instructions for producing a chemical reaction. In the late 1960s in France, a group of cultural historians led by Fernand Braudel became prominent. Collectively known as the "School of the Annales," these scholars looked at history as neither the parade of events nor the march of armies. Instead, they examined very specific things like the evolution of eating utensils and table manners, or the history of salt in the preservation of foods and how it affected the change of diets and empires across Europe. They looked at the importing of black pepper and other spices from India and the Spice Islands to Western Europe, and how that translated into the creation of great wealth for Portugal, Spain, the Netherlands, and finally Great Britain. Part of the Annales approach was to sort out the minutiae of everyday life—garbage, shopping lists, bills of lading from food purveyors, and so on—and, using these ordinary sources, create a revealing commentary on how larger social organizations formed or changed over time, whether it be a coffee shop, a neighborhood, or a nation. As a scholarly friend of mine points out, how perfectly appropriate it is that the country that gave us both Napoleon and Escoffier—both masters of detail and codification— should give us such a precise method for reflecting on our everyday surroundings: *Vive la logique!*

Following the Annales as a model, I use recipes as a window through which to catch a glimpse of a culture, whether our own or another. I start with the known and the familiar, and then expand to the slightly less familiar or, in some cases, the really unknown. This is how we learn about other cultures as well as about ourselves.

It is worth noting that many of the dishes in this book, regardless of their origin and history, are suited for the hectic pace of our Western style of living. They are prepared in one pot or skillet or casserole, and even though simmering times may be on the longish side, the pot in most cases can be left unattended. Some of these dishes also benefit from being prepared a day or two ahead, so flavors can develop and "mature."

As a final word, here's my advice for using this book. Think of it not as a collection of recipes too exotic for your own kitchen and pantry, but rather as a simple set of instructions for expanding on what you already know how to cook. And the bonus? An armchair glimpse into other cultures.

Some of the recipes in this collection create a special ethnic flavor by relying on specific ingredients that may require a brief explanation, which I present here. Ingredients marked with an asterisk may not be

notes
on ingredients

readily available; for those I've provided Ingredient Sources (page 199).

adobo

Depending on which country you're talking about, *adobo* can mean different things. The word *adobo* is Spanish, meaning a pickling sauce with vinegar and spices. In the Philippines, *adobo* is a very popular pork stew with vinegar. Alan Davidson in *The Oxford Companion to Food* suggests that when the Spaniards arrived in the Philippines, they tasted the Philippine pork stew, and since it reminded them of their own *adobado*, a pickled pork dish, they called it *adobo*. In Mexican cooking, *adobo* is a seasoning paste made of ground chiles and spices mixed with vinegar. Chipotle chiles (dried jalapeño chiles) are packaged in an *adobo* sauce made from this paste. In addition, you might find in the Hispanic food section of your supermarket a dry spice mixture called *adobo*.

banana leaves*

These leaves are pliable enough to wrap around foods for grilling, roasting, or steaming, and they impart a pleasant "grassy" flavor. Frozen banana leaves are available in one-pound packages. After thawing, wipe with a damp towel. Before using, soften by passing them over a hot burner or by dipping briefly in boiling water.

chiles*

There is evidence that chiles were first eaten in Mexico around 7000 B.C., and it is acknowledged that the Spanish and the Portuguese were responsible for transporting them to India and Southeast Asia, where previously black pepper had been the main source of tingling heat for the palate. The use of chiles eventually spread to the Balkans, the Middle East, and Europe.

aji: A hot chile grown in Peru and used extensively in home cooking throughout the country. There are many varieties, differing in size, shape, and intensity of spicy heat. Some are available in dried, powdered, and pickled forms.

ancho: This is a dried poblano chile, with a sweet medium-hot flavor that blends well in *moles* (chocolate-flavored chile sauces).

chipotle: When a large jalapeño chile is smoked and dried, it's called a chipotle and is often pickled or packed in cans with an *adobo* sauce. (See *Adobo*, above.)

fresno: This chile, developed in the 1950s in Fresno, California, ranges in color from yellowish green to bright red, and is slightly hotter than a jalapeño.

jalapeño: Probably the most familiar of the chiles in the U.S., its heat ranges from hardly noticeable to very hot, and its color from dark green to bright red.

pasilla: Almost black, with a medium-hot woodsy flavor, this chile is a fresh chilaca chile that has been dried. In the dried form, it's most often ground and used in sauces.

serrano: Usually green, this small, bullet-shaped chile is used extensively in Mexican cooking.

chinese black mushrooms, dried*

These are usually dried shiitake mushrooms, and are frequently used in Chinese simmered and braised dishes to add a meaty flavor and texture. There are several methods for softening them for cooking. Boiling water can be poured over them, and the mushrooms then allowed to soak for thirty minutes. Some cooks, including myself, think that soaking overnight in cold water results in a better texture.

chinese chestnuts, dried*

The Chinese use dried chestnuts for their sweet flavor and crumbly texture to offset the richness of simmered or braised meat dishes.

chinese five-spice powder

Blended from five spices (sometimes even more), the combination usually includes star anise, cloves, cinnamon, fennel, and Sichuan peppercorns. The number five has spiritual significance in many cultures, and for the Chinese it represents the five basic elements of the universe: earth, fire, metal, water, and wood.

chinese red dates, dried*

Also known as jujubes (no relation to the movie-theater candy), this date has been used in China for centuries in a variety of ways: in desserts and sweet soups; preserved with honey or salt; for ceremonial purposes, since its red color portends good fortune; and in braised meat dishes.

coconut juice*

Coconut juice is from a young coconut, usually with sugar added. Be sure not to confuse the juice (available canned) with coconut milk, which is much richer.

coconut milk

The velvety, rich milk extracted from the coconut nut is essential to the cooking of Southeast Asia. It is used to temper fiery curries (Indonesian Tuna Curry, page 120), add richness to soups and stews (Indian Vegetable Stew with Yogurt and Coconut, page 135), and lend creamy sweetness to desserts (Asian Black Rice Pudding, page 186).

Although some cooks will scoff at the use of canned coconut milk, the quality is usually quite good and saves time. Look for canned unsweetened coconut milk, and not the cream of coconut that is used for making piña coladas. Check the labels: Coconut and water should be the only ingredients, although a preservative may be listed after the water. Stay away from the "light" versions, since they frequently have an "off" taste.

fish sauce*

The Romans used fish sauce to flavor their food two thousand years ago, making it one of the earliest seasoning condiments. In Southeast Asia, fish sauce is used ubiquitously both in cooking and on the table—like salt in the United States and soy sauce in Japan. There is a different version of fish sauce in each country of that region: in Vietnam it is called *nuoc mam,* in Thailand *nam pla,* and in the Philippines *patis* (often called "fish gravy"). Although many people agree that the fish sauce "brewed" in Vietnam stands apart, one characteristic holds true for all of them: The aroma is stronger than the taste. Bruce Cost in his wonderful book *Asian Ingredients: A Guide to the Foodstuffs of China, Japan, Korean, Thailand and Vietnam,* compares the aroma to one's first whiff of Camembert cheese; it seems overpowering until you taste the subtle, layered flavors.

The care with which fish sauce is fermented is reminiscent of the painstaking process of making wine or olive oil. Small fish similar to anchovies are layered with salt in large wooden barrels and left to ferment for months. Then the liquid is drawn off through a spigot at the bottom of the barrel. Kept out of direct sunlight, fish sauce can be kept indefinitely.

lemongrass*

The taste of lemongrass is lemony and vaguely floral, and its flavor is found in many of the simmered dishes of Southeast Asia. Lemongrass looks like a wooden stalk, with a bulbous root end resembling a large scallion, and coarse greenish leaves. Usually lemongrass is used for flavoring, and then removed before the dish is served. Prepare lemongrass as you would a leek: trim the tough root end, peel the outer tough layers, and cut off the top green part, leaving five to six inches of the bulb end, which should be white to pale green in color. Bruise the stalk with the flat side of a chef's knife to release the flavor.

Select stalks that are fresh-looking, firm, smooth, and pale yellow-green. Refrigerate in a paper bag for several weeks, or freeze, well wrapped, up to six months. Lemongrass is available in a powdered form, but it usually has very little flavor. If you can't find the fresh, better to substitute two or three strips of lemon zest.

palm sugar*

Made from the sap of palm trees, this sugar has a flavor similar to that of maple sugar, and is used in the cooking of Southeast Asia not only in sweet dishes and desserts, but in savory dishes for balancing the saltiness of fish sauce, shrimp paste, and soy sauce and the "heat" of chiles. It can be found semisoft in plastic tubs or in hard logs or disks.

rice noodles, dried*

Also known as rice sticks, these noodles made from rice flour come in a variety of thicknesses; the medium-size is probably the best for soups, as in the Vietnamese Chicken Noodle Soup with Fresh Herbs (page 5).

shrimp paste or sauce*

The terms "shrimp paste" and "shrimp sauce" are often used interchangeably, and the package labeling sometimes adds to the confusion. But in either case, the product is made with shrimp that is salted and then fermented and dried. In the cooking of Southeast Asia, it is used to flavor a variety of dishes—including curries, casseroles, soups, fried rice, dipping sauces, and soups—and it adds protein, which is important in cuisines that are rice-based.

The shrimp mixture comes in two forms: a hard dried brick, and a soft-textured paste, ranging in color from pinkish lavender to gray—the paste is what I call for in this book. It is packaged in small plastic tubs and glass jars. Only a small amount is needed in a dish, and cooking is required to temper its flavor and odor. In Thailand, shrimp paste is called *kapi, kapee,* or *gkabpi,* and in Vietnam *mam ruoc* or *mam tom.* The Malaysian version is very thick and syrupy and slightly sweeter—almost like molasses—and is called *petis udang* (not to be confused with *patis,* the Philippine fish sauce).

soy sauce

Soy sauce is a seasoning created by the Chinese, who have cultivated soybeans for at least five thousand years. It is a salty liquid fermented from soybeans, wheat, salt, and a bacteria-based starter, and comes in three varieties: light, which has a delicate flavor and is perfect for seasoning chicken and seafood dishes and as a dipping sauce; medium or thin, which is saltier than the light, and is a good all-purpose sauce for cooking; and dark, often called superior, which has molasses added and gives a rich, slightly sweet flavor to simmered dishes and marinades.

Mushroom soy sauce* is a dark soy sauce that has been infused with the flavor of dried mushrooms, and when added to stews, it contributes a meaty, woodsy flavor.

Kecap manis * is a dark Indonesian soy sauce, sweetened with palm sugar and flavored with star anise and garlic.

star anise

A six- to eight-pointed starlike pod, this spice comes from a tree belonging to the magnolia family, and is grown in northern Vietnam and southern China. Its licorice flavor can be detected in much of the cooking of Southeast Asia. Remove from the dish before serving.

tamarind*

The tamarind tree produces a long, bean-shaped fruit pod that contains seeds and a sticky pulp. When the pulp, similar in flavor to a date, is processed, it yields a sour flavoring agent that is used in soups, stews, curries, and dipping sauces throughout Southeast Asia. Tamarind is commonly available in two forms for cooking: wrapped bricks of paste that contain seeds, and jars of strained concentrate. The latter is more convenient, since it can be used directly from the jar, although the paste imparts a fuller, deeper flavor to a dish. If tamarind is unavailable, substitute fresh lemon or lime juice on its own, or sweetened with a little brown sugar.

home cooking

poultry

One of the characteristics of Vietnamese cooking is the "brightness" of the aromatic flavor in many of the dishes. Fresh herbs and greens are often stirred in just before serving, as a kind of final garnish, and the heat of the dish releases their flavor and aroma.

vietnamese chicken noodle soup with fresh herbs

(pho ga)

MAKES 4 SERVINGS

Soups (*pho*) are a favorite in the food stalls, especially for breakfast. The chicken-noodle version that follows is in the tradition of chicken soups found in all cultures—and the simpler the better: water, chicken, maybe some vegetables, and noodles. In this instance, the noodles are flat Asian rice noodles. Aside from that variation, probably the most striking element that sets this recipe apart from all others you may have in your recipe collection is the handful of fresh herbs—cilantro, basil, and mint—that are stirred in just before serving.

1 1/2 pounds chicken thighs, on the bone
    and with skin
8 cups water
1/2 teaspoon salt
1/2 teaspoon coarse black pepper
2-inch piece fresh ginger, peeled, thinly sliced,
    and slices crushed with side of knife
1/2 cup sliced shallots (about 8 shallots) *or*
    thinly sliced scallions (about 4 scallions)
1/4 pound dried flat Asian rice noodles

garnishes
1 scallion, trimmed and thinly sliced
10 fresh cilantro sprigs
10 fresh basil sprigs
10 fresh mint sprigs
1 cup mung bean sprouts
Thinly sliced fresh red *or* green chile, seeded
    if less "heat" desired
Vietnamese fish sauce (*nuoc mam*)* *or*
    hoisin sauce
Hot chile oil

*For Ingredient Sources, see page 199.

In a large pot, combine the chicken thighs, water, salt, pepper, ginger, and shallots. Cover pot and bring to a boil. Lower heat and simmer, uncovered, until chicken is cooked through, 15 to 20 minutes. Using a slotted spoon, remove chicken from pot and set aside. Keep broth simmering.

Meanwhile, bring a large pot of water to a boil. Add the rice noodles and cook according to package directions. Drain, and then rinse under cold water. Set aside.

When chicken is cool enough to handle, remove skin and bones and discard them. Cut meat into small pieces. Arrange garnishes on a large platter.

Among 4 soup bowls, equally divide the chicken and noodles. Ladle the simmering chicken broth, including ginger and shallots, into each bowl. Let each diner select his or her own garnishes and stir them into the hot soup when first served, and as it is eaten.

I think I was about seven years old when I ate my first chicken pot pie. It was the frozen kind in a foil pan, heated up in the oven, and I loved the crust and the creamy filling. When I began to start cooking for myself in my early twenties, one of the first things I attempted was a chicken pot pie, and over the years it has evolved into the recipe that follows.

chicken pot pie with pecan–sour cream pastry

MAKES 6 SERVINGS

The real reason I like a pot pie is that it's just an excuse to have lots of flaky crust for dinner. The pastry here is especially rich, since it has four different kinds of fat: butter, vegetable shortening, sour cream, and ground nuts. (And as if this weren't enough, I've also added a little heavy cream to the filling.) In addition, the two "turns"—the rolling and folding of the pastry—and the initial high baking temperature, which sets the crust and creates pockets of steam, ensure even more flakiness.

To maximize flavor for the filling, I begin by poaching whole breasts on the bone, which produces a very rich broth.

Although there are a couple of different parts to the recipe, the techniques are simple and the result is delicious. I've been known to have eaten almost half of this pie at one sitting.

8

pastry

1½ cups all-purpose flour

1 teaspoon salt

Pinch sugar

6 tablespoons (¾ stick) unsalted butter,
  cut up and chilled

¼ cup solid vegetable shortening, cut up
  and chilled

2 tablespoons sour cream

2 tablespoons cold water, or more as needed

2 tablespoons ground pecans

filling

1 can (14.5 ounces) chicken broth

1 yellow onion, quartered

2 ribs celery, cut into 1-inch pieces

3 whole cloves

1 bay leaf

2½ pounds chicken breasts, on the bone

3 medium-size carrots, peeled and thickly sliced

1 cup frozen lima beans, thawed

1 cup frozen corn kernels, thawed

1 sweet red pepper, cored, seeded, and cut into
  medium dice

2 tablespoons unsalted butter

1 cup thinly sliced scallions (about 9 scallions)

5 tablespoons all-purpose flour

¼ teaspoon dried thyme

⅛ teaspoon ground allspice

½ cup heavy cream

1 teaspoon salt

⅛ teaspoon ground white pepper

pastry: In a food processor, combine the flour, salt, sugar, butter, and shortening. Pulse briefly, just until mixture is crumbly. Scrape mixture into a bowl. In a small cup, stir together the sour cream and water. Gradually add it to flour mixture, tossing with a fork until mixture comes together. If mixture is too dry, add more water, 1 teaspoon at a time, until dough comes together.

On a floured work surface, roll out dough into 10 × 5-inch rectangle. Sprinkle top evenly with 1 tablespoon ground pecans. Fold pastry into thirds like a business letter. Turn pastry so top opens like a book. Roll out again into 10 × 5-inch rectangle. Sprinkle top with remaining pecans. Fold into thirds again. Wrap dough in plastic wrap. Refrigerate at least 1 hour, or up to 2 days.

filling: In a saucepan just large enough to hold the chicken breasts, combine the chicken broth, onion, celery, cloves, and bay leaf. Add the chicken, and then enough cold water to barely cover chicken. Cover pan and bring liquid to a boil. Lower heat and simmer until chicken breasts are just cooked through, 10 to 15 minutes. Using a slotted spoon, remove chicken to a plate. Strain broth through a sieve into a bowl. Discard solids and return cooking liquid to saucepan.

Add the carrots to broth. Cover and bring to a boil. Boil 2 minutes. Add the lima beans, corn, and red pepper and boil another 2 minutes. Set a sieve over a bowl and drain vegetables, reserving broth. Spoon vegetables into a large bowl. Measure out 1½ cups of the broth. Refrigerate or freeze remaining liquid for soups.

In a large skillet, heat the butter over medium heat. Add the scallions and sauté until softened, about 4 minutes. Stir in the flour, thyme, and allspice. Cook gently 2 minutes, stirring occasionally. Stir in the

9

egg wash
1 egg
1 teaspoon milk

reserved 1½ cups broth. Boil gently, stirring, until thickened, about 5 minutes. Stir in the cream and boil gently until thickened, about 5 minutes. Add the salt and pepper. Remove from heat and set sauce aside.

Remove skin and bones from chicken and discard them. Cut meat into small cubes and add to vegetables in bowl. Fold in the sauce.

Heat oven to 450 degrees. Spoon the chicken filling into a 9 × 9 × 2-inch baking dish.

egg wash: In a small cup, stir together the egg and milk. On a floured surface, roll out dough ¼ inch thick. Cut into 10-inch square. Refrigerate scraps for other baking. Brush pastry with a little of the egg wash. Moisten edge of baking dish with water. Center pastry, egg side down, on top of baking dish. Gently press pastry to rim of dish and form stand-up edge. Brush pastry again with egg wash. Cut steam vents in pastry. Refrigerate 10 minutes.

Glaze pastry again with egg wash. Place pie in 450-degree oven. Immediately lower oven temperature to 400 degrees. Bake until pastry begins to brown, about 25 minutes. Lower heat to 350 degrees. Bake until pastry is crisp and golden brown, another 25 to 30 minutes. If edges of pastry begin to brown too quickly, cover loosely with foil. Let stand 15 minutes before serving.

make-ahead tip: The pot-pie filling as well as the pastry can be made earlier in the day. In fact, the whole pie can be assembled ahead, refrigerated, and then slipped into the oven about an hour before you plan to serve dinner.

If you were to pick one food that feeds most of the world, a top contender would be rice. I usually keep several kinds in my cupboard: basic white, jasmine, wild pecan, basmati, and Thai black sticky rice. Very often

chicken
with sausage and rice

(arroz con pollo)

MAKES 4 SERVINGS

dinner for me will be nothing more than a bowl of jasmine rice, sprinkled with a little Vietnamese fish sauce. It makes a simple but satisfying meal.

Chicken and rice is a combination that translates well from one part of the world to another. It's an economical way to stretch small quantities of meat and boost nutritional value, which is frequently the goal in home cooking. The recipe here has evolved from many versions I've sampled while traveling, both in home kitchens and in regional restaurants. Since I've always been partial to sausage, I toss in a few links. But the real core flavoring in this dish is the *adobo* that coats the chicken. (For a brief explanation of the culinary history of *adobo,* a method of seasoning as well as a seasoning mixture itself, see page xiii.)

adobo

3 tablespoons Oregano Spice Mixture
   (*recipe follows*)

3 cloves garlic, finely chopped

3 tablespoons cider vinegar

chicken, sausage, and rice

2 pounds whole chicken legs, split into
   drumsticks and thighs

2 tablespoons olive oil

1/2 pound hot Italian sausage, casings removed
   and sausage crumbled

1 small yellow onion, chopped

1 small sweet green pepper, cored, seeded,
   and chopped

1 teaspoon ground cumin

3 cloves garlic, chopped

1 cup medium-grain white rice

1 can (14.5 ounces) peeled whole tomatoes,
   with liquid, chopped

2 cans (14.5 ounces each) chicken broth

1 bay leaf

1 teaspoon dried oregano

1/4 teaspoon ground cinnamon

1 teaspoon salt

1/4 teaspoon black pepper

1 cup frozen green peas, thawed

2 tablespoons chopped pimiento-stuffed
   green olives

adobo: On a piece of waxed paper, spread the Oregano Spice Mixture. In a plastic food-storage bag, combine the garlic and vinegar.

chicken, sausage, and rice: Coat chicken with the spice mixture. Place in plastic bag with vinegar mixture. Seal bag and turn to coat chicken with liquid. Refrigerate at least 1 hour or overnight.

In a large skillet, heat oil over medium heat. Add the sausage and brown until fat is rendered out, 5 minutes. Using a slotted spoon, remove sausage to a plate. Pour off all but 1 tablespoon fat.

Add chicken to skillet and sauté over low heat until browned, 15 to 20 minutes, working in batches if necessary and being careful not to burn any pieces of garlic. As chicken browns, remove to a plate. Don't let bottom of skillet become too dark.

Add onion, pepper, and cumin to skillet and sauté until vegetables are softened, 4 to 5 minutes. Add garlic and sauté until fragrant, 1 minute. Stir in rice until coated but do not let brown. Stir in tomatoes with their liquid, chicken broth, bay leaf, oregano, cinnamon, salt, and pepper. Return chicken and sausage to skillet, adding water or more broth if needed to cover ingredients. Cover pan and bring to a boil. Lower heat and simmer until rice is tender and chicken is cooked through, 30 to 35 minutes. For last 5 minutes, stir in the peas. Remove from heat. Let stand, covered, 10 minutes.

Uncover skillet. If there is still excess liquid in skillet, cook over medium-high heat to evaporate. Remove bay leaf. Sprinkle with olives, and serve.

oregano spice mixture: In a small bowl, combine 1 tablespoon dried oregano, 1 tablespoon garlic powder, 1 tablespoon onion powder, 1 1/2 teaspoons salt, and 1 1/2 teaspoons black pepper.

13

In the Basque area of Spain, along the French border, this garlicky red pepper–ham sauce, known as *chilindron,* is one of the main flavoring elements in the gutsy cooking of the region. It's a cuisine that has not gotten much attention in this country, and I'm not sure why. I first traveled to the Basque region in the late 1960s, and found the rustic quality of the food very appealing, full of the kind of strong flavors in the chicken recipe that follows. When I crave some salt-cod fish cakes, *angulas* (baby eels) fried in oil, or other tapas from this part of Spain, I head for a restaurant called Pintxos—literally, "a pinch of food." There are only two Basque restaurants in New York City, and Pintxos is certainly the more home-style, both in style of food and in décor.

chicken legs in basque red pepper– prosciutto sauce

MAKES 4 SERVINGS

For a slightly Moroccan-Asian touch here, I've added Chinese five-spice powder, which is a blend of anise, ginger, cinnamon, and cloves. It accents in a deliciously subtle manner the flavor of both the prosciutto and the tomatoes.

The Basque sauce in this recipe can also be used in other ways. You can prepare it on its own and spoon it over rotelle or fusilli or any other pasta with "nooks and crannies" that will capture bits of the chunky sauce. Or spread it over slices of lightly toasted or grilled crusty bread for a meal-in-itself bruschetta.

14

2 tablespoons olive oil

3 pounds whole chicken legs, split into
   drumsticks and thighs

1/2 teaspoon salt

sauce

1 can (1 pound, 12 ounces) peeled whole
   tomatoes plus 1 can (14.5 ounces) peeled
   whole tomatoes

2 teaspoons olive oil

2 yellow onions, chopped

4 cloves garlic, finely chopped

2 sweet red peppers, cored, seeded, and cut
   into large dice

1/4 pound thick-sliced good-quality prosciutto *or*
   smoked ham, cut into 1/2-inch cubes

2 tablespoons brandy

1 bay leaf

1 teaspoon dried thyme

1 teaspoon Chinese five-spice powder

3/4 teaspoon salt

1/2 teaspoon dried basil

1/4 teaspoon black pepper

In a large skillet, heat the oil. Season the chicken with the salt and add to skillet. Working in batches if necessary to avoid crowding skillet, brown chicken on all sides, about 20 minutes. Remove chicken to a plate as it browns. Drain off fat from skillet.

Heat oven to 350 degrees.

sauce: Drain the tomatoes over a bowl, reserving liquid. In same skillet, heat the oil. Add the onion and sauté until slightly softened, about 4 minutes. Add the garlic, sweet pepper, and prosciutto and sauté until sweet pepper is slightly softened, about 5 minutes. Add the brandy and cook briefly, scraping up any browned bits from bottom of skillet, until most of liquid has evaporated, about 2 minutes. Add drained tomatoes, breaking up with a wooden spoon. Mixture should be moist but not too liquid. If too wet, cook a little more. If too dry, add a little of reserved tomato liquid. Add the bay leaf, thyme, five-spice powder, salt, basil, and black pepper. Spoon into a 13 × 9 × 2-inch baking dish or casserole. Tuck chicken pieces into sauce, spooning some sauce over chicken. Cover dish tightly with aluminum foil.

Bake in 350-degree oven until instant-read thermometer inserted into thickest part of legs and thighs without touching bone registers 170 degrees, about 45 minutes. For the last 10 minutes of baking, uncover the dish and increase oven temperature to 400 degrees. When cooked, transfer chicken to a platter. If sauce has become too thin, spoon into saucepan and cook until thickened. Spoon over chicken, and serve.

serving tip: Accompany with rice or noodles.

Eating at food stalls in Southeast Asia is an easy and inexpensive way to learn about the region's wonderful cuisine. The food is all laid out, and can be quickly assembled by the vendor. Language is no problem—just point and smile. But it does pay to exercise common sense: if the food looks a little "tired," move on. A friend I often travel with has two rules about eating on the street: First, make sure there are at least three people already eating there. And second, check that the dishes are being washed in a large pan of hot water, with lots of soap suds. So far, I've never had any problems eating at these stalls.

thai green curry with chicken and green beans

(kaeng khiaw-waan)

MAKES 4 SERVINGS

When traveling with the same friend in Thailand, his favorite dish to order was green curry. After our twenty-third stall stop, we began to become experts on the subtleties of green curry versus red. This is my version of Thai green curry. Thai curries are usually made quickly, keeping the flavor very fresh and light, and the finished dish is brothy. The meat is not browned first, but added raw to the pot, making preparation even quicker. What gives this kind of curry its spicy heat are fresh chiles, which did not appear in Southeast Asia until the 1500s, when the Portuguese brought them from the New World. Prior to that time, black pepper provided the palate tingle.

The recipe for making a green curry paste from scratch is included here, but you can substitute a ready-to-use green curry paste, available in the Asian section of some supermarkets, in specialty food shops, or from the Ingredient Sources listed in the back of this book (see page 199). For these curry pastes, the spices are often toasted in a dry skillet for a deeper, more pungent flavor. I omit that step here, but it's quite easy to do. Just toss the spices in a dry skillet over medium heat until they color slightly and become aromatic.

16

green curry paste

8 small fresh green chiles, cored, seeded,
    and chopped (for extra "heat," leave the
    seeds in)

1 medium-size yellow onion, chopped

6 tablespoons chopped fresh cilantro

1 tablespoon chopped garlic

1 tablespoon chopped, peeled fresh ginger

2 teaspoons ground coriander

1 teaspoon ground cumin

1 tablespoon coarse black pepper

1 teaspoon Thai shrimp paste (*kapi*)*

chicken

2 tablespoons vegetable oil

2 cloves garlic, finely chopped

1 can (14 ounces) coconut milk

3 tablespoons sugar

3 tablespoons Thai fish sauce (*nam pla*)*

1 cup chicken broth

1/4 pound green beans, trimmed, and left whole
    or cut into 1-inch pieces

1 pound boneless, skinless chicken thighs,
    cut into small chunks *or* thin pieces

Grated zest of 1 lime (about 2 teaspoons)

*For Ingredient Sources, see page 199.

green curry paste: In a small food processor, combine the chiles, onion, cilantro, garlic, ginger, coriander, cumin, black pepper, and shrimp paste. Process to make a paste. (Or if you have a stone mortar and pestle, mash the ingredients together using that.) Scrape into a jar and store in the refrigerator for up to 1 week, or freeze for up to a month.

chicken: In a large skillet, heat the oil. Add the garlic and sauté until lightly golden, about 2 minutes. Stir in 3 tablespoons of the Green Curry Paste and cook for 30 seconds. Stir in the coconut milk and gently boil until slightly thickened, 3 to 5 minutes. Stir in the sugar and fish sauce. Stir in the chicken broth. Stir in the green beans and simmer until slightly tender, about 4 minutes. Stir in the chicken and gently simmer until cooked through, about 10 minutes. Stir in the lime zest, and serve.

serving tip: White rice or jasmine rice is a usual accompaniment to this dish.

Ají is a particular chile grown in Peru. There are several different kinds, and they can be found fresh in this country in Peruvian markets and pickled in jars in grocery stores specializing in Spanish ingredients. If they're not available, substitute red Fresno chiles or jalapeños. Like *Papas a la Huancaina* (page 141), there are many versions of this spicy chicken dish, depending on where you are in Peru. Perhaps the most well known are from Callao and Chiclayo.

peruvian chicken in walnut-and-pepper sauce

(ají de pollo)

MAKES 6 SERVINGS

The sauce for this dish is thickened with ground walnuts, bread crumbs softened in evaporated milk, and grated Parmesan cheese. Once the shredded chicken is added, it's spooned over sliced cooked potatoes, for a warming, hearty dish.

1 cup fresh bread crumbs

1 cup evaporated milk

2½ pounds chicken parts, such as drumsticks, thighs, and breasts

2 cans (14.5 ounces each) chicken broth

1½ pounds Yukon Gold potatoes *or* other boiling potato, with skins on

6 fresh ají chiles, red Fresno chiles, *or* other red chiles, cored and seeded

1 tomato, cored and chopped

1 tablespoon vegetable oil

2 yellow onions, chopped

3 cloves garlic, finely chopped

¼ pound walnuts, ground

1 teaspoon salt

¼ teaspoon black pepper

¼ cup orange juice

¼ cup grated Parmesan cheese

In a small bowl, soak the bread crumbs in the evaporated milk.

In a large saucepan, combine the chicken parts and chicken broth, adding water if needed to cover chicken. Cover pan and bring broth to a boil. Lower heat and simmer until chicken is tender and cooked through, about 30 minutes. Remove saucepan from heat. Remove chicken from liquid and let cool slightly. Reserve the cooking liquid.

Meanwhile, in a large pot of lightly salted boiling water, cook the potatoes until fork-tender, about 25 minutes. Then drain.

When chicken is cool enough to handle, remove skin and bones from chicken and discard them. Shred meat into 1½ × ¼-inch pieces. With a fork, mash the softened bread crumbs in the milk. In a small food processor or blender, puree together the chiles and tomato.

In a large skillet, heat the oil. Add the onion and sauté until softened, about 5 minutes. Add the garlic and sauté 1 minute. Stir in the bread crumb mixture, then the chile mixture until well blended. Stir in the ground walnuts. Add the salt and pepper. Cook over medium heat about 5 minutes, stirring frequently to prevent scorching on bottom of pot. Add the shredded chicken and ½ cup of its reserved cooking liquid, the orange juice, and the Parmesan. Heat through, stirring. Keep warm.

Drain the potatoes. Slice and arrange on a platter. Pour the hot chicken mixture over top, and serve.

Here's one of those recipes with a folk history that changes slightly, depending on who you're talking to and where they're from—there is a Brunswick County, Virginia; a Brunswick, Georgia; and a Brunswick, North Carolina. In 1828, one story goes, Dr. Creed Haskins, a member of the Virginia legislature, was hosting a political rally for the Democratic Party's presidential candidate, Andrew Jackson. To feed the guests,

brunswick stew
with chicken

Dr. Haskins had his cook, Jimmy Matthews, re-create the stew they frequently cooked up at the end of a day of hunting—and that's what became known as Brunswick Stew. But regardless of its true origin, the dish is clearly a backwoods creation. Early recipes include squirrel and sometimes rabbit and bird, as well as corn and often lima beans and potatoes. These days, cooks omit the wildlife and substitute chicken, pork, or beef, or any combination thereof. If you've spooned up a bowlful of this stew in Kentucky, chances are it's called a burgoo. And to make matters even more confusing, there's a similar dish in South Carolina called perloo or pilau, as well as its distant cousin jambalaya in Louisiana.

In any event, wander the back roads in Virginia during the fall, and you'll probably come across church suppers and other community fund-raisers where Brunswick Stew is featured on the menu. The flavor of the stew is classic sweet and sour, which comes from the same elements one finds in Southern barbecue: tomato and vinegar with a little brown sugar. It's a flavor combination that has wide appeal. For example, Filipinos and Indonesians balance sour tamarind with sweet coconut, and the Vietnamese mix fish sauce with caramel. In all these instances, the palate of flavors is similar, but how you get there is what determines the personality of each dish.

21

poultry

1 chicken (3 to 4 pounds), cut into pieces

4 scallions, trimmed and sliced

2 carrots, trimmed, peeled, and thickly sliced

2 bay leaves

1 teaspoon dried thyme

1 teaspoon salt

1/4 teaspoon black pepper

Cold water

1/3 cup ketchup

3 tablespoons cider vinegar

1 tablespoon packed dark-brown sugar

2 cups corn kernels, fresh *or* frozen

1 package (10 ounces) frozen baby lima beans

1 can (14.5 ounces) peeled whole tomatoes,
   with liquid, chopped

1 piece (6 ounces) smoked ham, such as
   Black Forest, diced (optional)

1 teaspoon Worcestershire sauce

1/4 teaspoon liquid hot-pepper seasoning

In a large pot, place the chicken, scallions, carrots, bay leaves, thyme, salt, and pepper. Add enough cold water to just cover chicken. Bring to a boil. Gently simmer, partially covered, until chicken meat just about falls off the bones, 1 1/2 to 2 hours. Using a slotted spoon, remove chicken to a platter and let cool slightly.

Drain cooking liquid through a colander set over a large bowl. Discard solids. Rinse out cooking pot and colander. Line colander with a double thickness of dampened paper towels. Strain cooking liquid through colander placed over a clean bowl. Pour liquid back into pot. Boil until reduced to 4 to 5 cups.

In small bowl, stir together the ketchup, vinegar, and brown sugar. Stir into cooking liquid in pot. Add the corn, frozen lima beans, and tomatoes with their liquid, and the ham, if using. Bring to a boil. Lower heat and simmer until vegetables are tender, about 20 minutes.

When chicken is cool enough to handle, remove skin and bones and discard them. Shred meat into small pieces, and add to pot. Gently heat through. Then season with the Worcestershire and hot-pepper seasoning. Sample a spoonful, and then adjust the seasonings to your own taste. Serve.

serving tip: A basket of warm, home-baked biscuits is the perfect addition.

This dish is perhaps best described as a marriage of Normandy with New England—the French apples and cream turn slightly pink when they encounter the New England cranberry, and the mustard and grated orange rind boost the sweet-sour flavor. One friend has dubbed this preparation "Thanksgiving in a skillet."

There was a time when the only thing I ever cooked, even for dinner guests, was this kind of quick skillet sauté with its own rich pan sauce. I'd prep all my ingredients ahead of time, and then I could both cook and chat at the same time as I quickly assembled the sauté.

skillet chicken with apples and cranberries

MAKES 4 SERVINGS

2 tablespoons unsalted butter

1 tablespoon vegetable oil

4 boneless, skinless chicken breast halves
    (about 1½ pounds total)

½ teaspoon salt

¼ teaspoon white pepper

2 shallots, chopped

2 Granny Smith apples, peeled, halved, cored,
    seeded, and cut into ¼-inch-thick wedges

1 cup cranberries, fresh *or* frozen, thawed

⅓ cup chicken broth

¾ cup heavy cream

2 teaspoons grated orange zest

2 teaspoons Dijon mustard

Chopped toasted pecans, walnuts, almonds, *or*
    macadamia nuts, for garnish (optional)

In a large skillet, heat the butter and oil over medium-high heat. Season the chicken with the salt and white pepper. Add chicken to skillet and sauté until lightly browned, about 6 minutes. Turn breasts over and sauté another 6 to 8 minutes or until lightly browned and cooked through, covering skillet for the last 2 minutes. Remove chicken to a plate and cover with foil to keep warm.

Pour off all but about 1 tablespoon of the fat in skillet. Add the shallots and sauté 1 minute. Add the apple wedges and cranberries and sauté 1 minute. Add the chicken broth and scrape up any browned bits from bottom of skillet. Cover skillet with foil and cook for 1 to 2 minutes or until apple wedges are slightly tender. Uncover and continue to cook until liquid begins to become syrupy. Pour in the cream and gently boil until liquid thickens and a wooden spoon dragged across bottom of skillet leaves a track. Stir in the orange zest and mustard. Return chicken to skillet and gently heat, if needed. To garnish, scatter the nuts over the top, if using, and serve.

serving tip: Accompany with couscous, white rice, or wild pecan rice.

25

poultry

This classic Moroccan dish was probably first introduced to many Americans by Paula Wolfert, who through her books has done much to popularize the cooking of that part of the world. My simplified version calls for strips of orange zest rather than the more traditional preserved lemons, and I use a Dutch oven or heavy oven-proof casserole instead of the tagine, the cone-shaped clay pot usually used for cooking the stew.

mediterranean chicken stew with prunes and almonds

MAKES 4 SERVINGS

During the early stages of tinkering with the recipe, I invited a friend who knows Morocco well to taste what I had cooked. After eating a spoonful he nodded his approval, but asked where the nuts were—that's how the almonds found their way into this particular recipe. If you can, use Yukon Gold potatoes; because of their buttery flavor, they add richness to the sauce.

Definitely try to let the stew stand at least an hour before serving, since the starch from the potato will thicken the stew. Even better, serve it the next day—the sweet spices and the prunes will have blended to create rich undertones.

3 pounds chicken thighs, on the bone, with
skin removed

1 tablespoon olive oil

1 small yellow onion, chopped

1 can (14.5 ounces) chicken broth

3 cloves garlic, chopped

2 tablespoons chopped, peeled fresh ginger

1 tablespoon ground cumin

2 teaspoons Hungarian sweet paprika

1 teaspoon ground cardamom

1 teaspoon salt

½ teaspoon black pepper

3 strips orange zest

2 bay leaves

1 pound baby Yukon Gold potatoes *or* other
boiling potatoes, unpeeled, and halved or
quartered, depending on size

1 cup pitted green olives

1 cup pitted prunes, halved lengthwise

½ cup slivered or sliced almonds *or* chopped
pistachios

½ cup finely chopped fresh flat-leaf parsley

½ cup chopped fresh mint

In a large Dutch oven or casserole, sauté the chicken in the oil until lightly browned on all sides, 10 to 15 minutes, working in batches if necessary to avoid crowding the pan. As it browns, remove chicken to a platter.

Add the onion to the pot and sauté, adding a little chicken broth as needed to scrape up any browned bits from bottom of pot, until onion is softened, about 10 minutes. Add the garlic and sauté for 1 minute. Stir in the ginger, cumin, paprika, cardamom, salt, and black pepper and cook 1 minute, stirring occasionally.

Stir in remaining chicken broth. Add the orange zest and bay leaves. Return chicken to pot, and add the potatoes, olives, prunes, and nuts. Add enough water to make sure everything is covered by liquid. Cover and bring to a boil. Lower heat and simmer, with lid slightly askew, for 45 minutes or until potatoes are tender and chicken meat is practically falling off the bone. Occasionally skim foam from surface and discard.

Stir the parsley and mint into pot. Simmer another 5 minutes. Remove bay leaves and zest and discard. Serve the stew in small bowls or wide, shallow soup bowls.

serving tip: Slices of pita bread spread with a tapenade make a rich complement.

It's rumored that a Filipino friend of mine who lives in San Francisco is famous for the communion wafers he bakes for his local church. He is in fact a great baker as well as a terrific cook. It's not unusual for him to have a pot of ham hocks or whatever simmering on his stove's back burner. This recipe came from him, and he got it from his mother. A standard in the Philippine repertoire of home cooking, this soup, known as *sinigang,* derives its distinctive tart-sour flavor from tamarind and its saltiness from *patis,* the Philippine fermented fish sauce—two flavors characteristic of Philippine cooking.

philippine sour soup with chicken

(sinigang)

MAKES 4 SERVINGS

There are as many different versions of *sinigang* as there are cooks who make it, which is usually the case with dishes that are part of the everyday cuisine. As a result, this soup can be prepared with boneless pork cutlets, beef tenderloin, fish, shellfish, or chicken cutlets; the version here uses chicken. And like so many home-cooked, one-pot dishes in Southeast Asia, the meat is not browned first, as it would often be in Western cooking. Water, rather than broth, is the cooking medium, and ingredients are added according to their cooking times. This is a quick-cooking, brothy soup, so the flavors remain very fresh.

29

6 cups cold water

1 large yellow onion, halved and thinly
   sliced crosswise

2 medium-size tomatoes, cored and cut
   into cubes

$3/4$ pound green beans, trimmed and cut into
   1-inch pieces

2 fresh jalapeño chiles, cored, seeded, and
   chopped

1 tablespoon Philippine fish sauce (*patis*)* *or*
   other fish sauce

$1/4$ cup tamarind concentrate*

1 pound boneless, skinless chicken breasts,
   cut into thin strips

1 pound leafy greens, such as spinach or
   Swiss chard, stemmed and cleaned

*For Ingredient Sources, see page 199.

In a large pot, bring 6 cups of water to a boil. Add the onion and tomatoes and simmer for 5 minutes. Add the green beans, jalapeño, fish sauce, and tamarind concentrate and simmer about 3 minutes to blend flavors. Add the chicken and simmer until cooked through, about 10 minutes.

Stir in the leafy greens. Remove pot from heat and cover it. Let stand until greens are wilted, about 5 minutes. Spoon the soup into large shallow soup bowls, and serve.

serving tips: A fruit salad with mango or papaya makes a sweet counterpoint to the tart flavor of the soup. This soup is also delicious chilled. For a vegetarian alternative, substitute tofu for the chicken.

If I even whisper the word "chicken" to my Peruvian friend Anki, his eyes light up. Peruvians seem to have a special relationship with poultry dishes. One of the most popular in Peru, as well as among the transplanted Peruvian populations in the United States, is a whole chicken roasted with a blend of lively spices. Another Peruvian favorite is this chicken stew, in which pieces of chicken are simmered in a broth along with sweet potatoes and a sprinkling of sweet spices—cumin and allspice.

peruvian chicken stew with sweet potatoes and peanuts

MAKES 6 SERVINGS

In the Peruvian kitchen, one of the characteristic techniques for thickening broth is to stir in ground nuts and/or cornmeal toward the end of the cooking time. This is perhaps a kitchen trick borrowed from African cooking, of which there are many influences in Peruvian cooking, since from the seventeenth to the nineteenth century landowners imported African slaves to work the land. In the European kitchen, a cook would thicken the broth with flour or, in some cases, cornstarch or arrowroot.

31

2 tablespoons vegetable oil

1½ pounds chicken thighs, on the bone,
   with skin removed

1 yellow onion, halved lengthwise and thinly
   sliced crosswise

6 cups water *or* canned chicken broth

1 teaspoon salt

1 teaspoon ground cumin

1 cup dry-roasted, unsalted peanuts, ground
   medium-fine

½ cup yellow cornmeal

⅛ teaspoon ground allspice

1 pound sweet potatoes, peeled and cut into
   2 × ¼ × ¼-inch sticks

¼ cup chopped fresh cilantro (optional)

In a large saucepan or Dutch oven, heat the oil over medium heat. Add the chicken thighs and slowly brown on all sides, about 20 minutes. Remove chicken thighs to a plate.

Add the onion to the pot and sauté over low heat until softened, about 10 minutes; do not let onion brown. Return chicken thighs to the pot. Add the water, salt, and cumin. Bring to a boil. Then lower heat and simmer, uncovered, until chicken is very tender, 30 to 40 minutes.

Stir in the ground peanuts, cornmeal, and allspice and cook 15 minutes, scraping bottom of pot occasionally to prevent scorching. Stir in the sweet potato sticks and cook 15 to 20 minutes or until sweet potato is tender and mixture is very thick. If you like the flavor of cilantro, stir that in just before serving. Spoon the stew into serving bowls.

serving tip: Accompany with cubes of papaya tossed with fresh lime juice and spooned over a bed of leafy lettuce.

beef

When I was growing up, we called this dish Swiss steak and we had it with great regularity. You'll often see the same dish on a restaurant menu, but it's called braised beef. When meat is braised, it's slowly cooked with a little liquid in a covered pot, a technique that is ideal for tenderizing tougher cuts of meat and making them meltingly tender, with the added bonus of the tasty sauce that's automatically created at the same time. Home cooking in many cuisines is characterized by this technique. Here, the recipe also includes

braised beef with oregano and cardamom

MAKES 4 SERVINGS

another technique that coaxes the flavorful juices from ingredients, and it's aptly called "sweating." In this case, chopped vegetables are slowly cooked in a covered pot until they're stewing in their own natural liquid.

By adding cardamom to the flour mixture and a cinnamon stick to the cooking liquid, I've slightly "sweetened" the flavor of the version that I remember from childhood. For a more intense flavor, I sometimes add two or three lightly crushed cardamom pods to the pot.

To double the recipe, use a four-pound roast, double the amount of ingredients in the flour-dredging mixture, and increase the chicken broth to one 14.5-ounce can and the tomato paste to 2 tablespoons.

1 yellow onion, cut into quarters

3 carrots, trimmed, peeled, and cut into
1-inch pieces

2 ribs celery, trimmed and cut into 1-inch pieces

4 cloves garlic, peeled

1/4 cup all-purpose flour

1 teaspoon ground cardamom

1/2 teaspoon salt

1/4 teaspoon black pepper

2 pounds beef bottom round *or* round steak,
about 1 inch thick

2 tablespoons vegetable oil

1 cup chicken broth

1 tablespoon tomato paste

3/4 teaspoon dried oregano

2 bay leaves

1 cinnamon stick

Heat oven to 325 degrees. In a food processor, chop together the onion, carrots, celery, and garlic. On a piece of waxed paper, mix together the flour, cardamom, salt, and pepper. Dredge the beef in the flour mixture to coat well on all sides. In a Dutch oven or ovenproof casserole, heat the oil over medium-high heat. Add beef and quickly brown on both sides, about 6 minutes total. Remove beef to a platter and cover with foil to keep warm.

To the pot, add the chopped onion mixture. Lower heat, cover pot, and cook, stirring occasionally, until vegetables release their juices and are softened but not colored, about 8 minutes. Stir in the chicken broth, tomato paste, oregano, bay leaves, and cinnamon stick. Return beef to pot and spoon liquid over top of beef.

Cover pot and bake in 325-degree oven until beef is very tender, 2 to 2 1/2 hours. Check from time to time, basting the meat and making sure there is still a little liquid in bottom of pot. The sauce will get thicker as cooking continues.

Remove meat to a platter and keep warm. Remove bay leaves and cinnamon stick and discard. Skim fat from surface of sauce. Ladle sauce over beef, and serve.

serving tips: A delicious "boat" for the sauce can be made with mashed turnips, mashed celery root, mashed white potatoes, or mashed sweet potatoes, or a combination of these. If there are meat leftovers, thinly slice the meat for sandwiches.

In most places in South America or in Cuba you'll run across a version of this hearty dish. Its common name in Spanish is *ropa vieja,* which means "old clothes." Since the meat is shredded to resemble tattered rags, flank steak is the best choice because of its coarse grain. Think of this dish as a kind of American hash with potatoes. Peruvians, in fact, will often top their shredded beef with a fried egg.

shredded flank steak with potatoes and chiles

MAKES 6 SERVINGS

Simmering the steak first in a flavored broth creates richness and depth of flavor in the finished dish. Star anise, a spice often used in the cuisine of Vietnam and southern China, adds a slightly Asian note. You can stop after removing the meat from the broth, and treat the steak as a boiled dinner, serving the broth on the side or as a first course. But if you follow the recipe to the end, you'll never think of "meat and potatoes" the same way again.

1 dried pasilla chile, stemmed and seeded

Hot water

1 yellow onion, cut into quarters

2 whole cloves garlic, peeled and slightly crushed

2 stalks celery, cut into 2-inch lengths

1 bay leaf

3 pieces star anise

3 teaspoons salt

1 flank steak (about 1½ pounds)

1 can (14.5 ounces) chicken broth

1 pound boiling potatoes, peeled

1 or 2 red Fresno chiles or other red chiles,
    cored, seeded, and chopped

2 tablespoons vegetable oil

2 yellow onions, chopped

2 cloves garlic, chopped

2 tablespoons chopped fresh cilantro or parsley,
    for garnish

In a small bowl, soak the dried pasilla chile in enough hot water to cover, 1 hour. Drain.

Meanwhile, in a large pot, combine the quartered onion, whole cloves garlic, celery, bay leaf, star anise, 2 teaspoons salt, and flank steak. Add the chicken broth and enough cold water to cover ingredients. Cover pot and bring to a boil. Lower heat and simmer, partially covered, until very tender, about 1½ hours. Remove steak. When cool enough to handle, shred meat along grain, using your hands or a knife.

Remove the other solids from the broth and discard. Add the potatoes to broth and boil until knife-tender, about 30 minutes. Drain, reserving cooking liquid. When cool enough to handle, cut potatoes into 1-inch cubes.

In a small blender or food processor, combine the dried pasilla chile, fresh chiles, and ¼ cup reserved cooking liquid. Process until smooth.

In a large skillet, heat the oil. Add the chopped onion and sauté until softened, about 8 minutes. Add the chopped garlic and sauté 1 minute. Add the chile mixture and cook 1 minute. Add the shredded meat and remaining 1 teaspoon salt and cook over low heat 3 to 5 minutes, for meat to absorb flavors. Add potatoes and heat through. If mixture at any point becomes too dry, add a little of the cooking liquid. Garnish with chopped cilantro or parsley, and serve.

Wherever you find a chicken in a barnyard or outside on a front stoop, you're likely to find a hard-cooked egg somewhere in that country's cuisine. This is true for South America, Southeast Asia, Eastern Europe, and North Africa. In this recipe for pot roast, strongly influenced by the seasonings of Morocco, whole eggs in the shell are simmered right alongside the meat. To make the eggs slightly darker on the inside for a visual effect, after the first hour of cooking—when the eggs have become firm—gently crack the shells.

moroccan pot roast with apricots and hard-cooked eggs

MAKES 6 SERVINGS

The sweet spices—ginger, cinnamon, nutmeg—are a natural complement to the sweet apricots and raisins, and, in addition, they infuse the meat and its accompaniments with a rich, exotic flavor.

beef

1 medium-size yellow onion, chopped

4 cloves garlic, chopped

1/4 cup golden raisins

1/4 cup dried pitted apricots, chopped

1/2 teaspoon ground ginger

1/2 teaspoon ground cinnamon

1/2 teaspoon ground nutmeg

1/2 teaspoon ground turmeric

1/2 teaspoon salt

1/2 teaspoon black pepper

1 beef bottom round *or* chuck roast
    (about 2 pounds), trimmed of excess fat

2 sweet potatoes *or* yams, peeled and cut
    into 3/4-inch cubes

6 eggs in their shells, at room temperature

2 cans (14.5 ounces each) chicken broth, or
    more as needed

1 can (15 ounces) chickpeas, drained and rinsed

garnishes

Thinly sliced scallions

Grated orange zest

Heat oven to 300 degrees. In a Dutch oven or casserole, stir together the onion, garlic, raisins, apricots, ginger, cinnamon, nutmeg, turmeric, salt, and pepper and spread the mixture evenly over bottom of pot. Place the meat on top of onion mixture. Arrange the sweet potatoes and the eggs in their shells around roast. Pour in the broth, gently pushing eggs down so they are almost submerged. Add a little more broth if needed. Cover pot and bring to a simmer on stovetop.

Place pot in 300-degree oven and bake, covered, until the meat is very tender, about 2 hours. Check occasionally to make sure eggs remain almost submerged, adding more broth as needed. Stir in the chickpeas for the last 30 minutes of cooking.

Remove pot from oven. Transfer roast and hard-cooked eggs to cutting board, and re-cover pot. When eggs are cool enough to handle, remove shells and slice eggs. Slice meat and place in bottom of large soup bowls. Spoon broth with sweet potatoes, dried fruit, and chickpeas over meat. Garnish with sliced egg, scallion, and orange zest, and serve. This is a knife-and-fork-and-spoon dish.

Many of the recipes in this chapter use secondary or tougher, inexpensive cuts of beef that benefit from a long simmer to tenderize the meat and develop its wonderful flavor. What follows is an example from the opposite end of the scale: a very tender cut of beef— the fillet—that is poached for a very short time. The fillet is an expensive cut, but there is absolutely no waste. This recipe is really the French *boeuf à la ficelle* (beef on a string), a very simple, elegant dish. The roast is suspended in the poaching liquid by a string from either end. While many of the other beef recipes in this chapter have a complex range of flavors, this one is the simplest of "boiled" dinners, in which the flavor of the rich cut of meat is subtly accented by the cooking liquid.

french beef on a string with sour cream— horseradish sauce

MAKES 6 SERVINGS

The horseradish sauce is based on one I learned about twenty-five years ago, when I worked in the kitchens of Donald Bruce White, a New York City caterer. Donald was a Dorian Gray sort of character, forever boyish. His choreographed events, whether intimate or grand, always included black-tie waiters hand-picked for their Cary Grant looks.

beef

2 cans (14.5 ounces each) chicken broth *or*
    homemade chicken stock

6 cups cold water

1 leek, trimmed, cut into 2-inch lengths,
    washed, and halved, *or* 1 yellow onion,
    cut into wedges

1 carrot, trimmed, peeled, and cut into
    2-inch lengths

1 rib celery, trimmed and cut into 2-inch lengths

2 cloves garlic, crushed

2 bay leaves

1/2 teaspoon dried thyme

2 whole cloves

2 to 2 1/2 pounds beef fillet *or* boneless
    rib-eye roast

sauce

1/2 cup heavy cream

3/4 cup sour cream

2 tablespoons bottled horseradish, drained

1/3 cup finely chopped toasted walnuts

1/2 teaspoon salt

beef: In a pot large enough to hold the beef fillet so it can be suspended in the cooking liquid, combine the chicken broth, water, leek, carrot, celery, garlic, bay leaves, thyme, and cloves. Bring to a boil. Reduce the heat and simmer, partially covered, 30 minutes to develop the flavor of the broth.

Meanwhile, tie the fillet at 2-inch intervals, if not already done so by the butcher. Attach a string to either end of the roast, making the ends long enough so they overhang the side of pot. Lower meat into simmering liquid, cover the pot, and gently simmer until an instant-read thermometer inserted in thickest part of meat registers about 130 degrees for medium rare, 20 to 25 minutes. Remove the fillet to a platter, cover with aluminum foil, and let stand 15 minutes (the internal temperature will increase as fillet stands). Strain cooking liquid and refrigerate or freeze for future use; or serve the broth as a light first course (see Serving Tip below).

sauce: While beef is cooking, beat the cream in a medium-size bowl until soft peaks form. Gently fold in the sour cream, horseradish, walnuts, and salt. Cover and refrigerate until ready to serve.

After the beef has rested, remove string. Slice beef somewhat thickly and serve warm or at room temperature with horseradish sauce.

serving tip: As with many boiled dinners, the rich, flavorful cooking liquid can be served as a first-course broth, and since the vegetables have not been overcooked, they make for a simple garnish.

beef

Beef and carrots in a stew may reflect heartland America in many people's minds, but in this chapter, those same ingredients also appear in a classic Vietnamese dish (page 48) as well as in the Belgian rendition here—it's the seasonings that account for the exciting differences in flavor.

flemish carbonnade with carrots

MAKES 6 SERVINGS

You may have noticed the word "carbon" in the name "carbonnade," and most authorities agree that originally there was a charcoal connection. Beef, whether small pieces or a large chunk, was first grilled over a charcoal fire, then braised or slowly simmered in a broth to produce a stew. Here, rather than grilling the meat, it is well browned in a pot in order to caramelize the natural sugars and develop a richer flavor. The Vietnamese also like the caramel taste in many of their dishes, which derives from their use of sugar, and for even fuller flavor, they stir in fish sauce. In this recipe, beer—for which Belgium is famous—adds the same kind of fullness, and slowly sautéed onions color the stew with sweetness. If you've never cooked with beer before, two bottles may seem excessive—but remember, most of the alcohol cooks away, leaving a robust "beefy" taste.

46

4 tablespoons (½ stick) unsalted butter

1 tablespoon vegetable oil, or more as needed

6 medium-size Vidalia onions *or* other sweet
   onions, sliced

3 cloves garlic, finely chopped

1 beef bottom round roast (2 pounds), trimmed
   and cut into ½-inch cubes

2 bottles (12 ounces each) dark beer

6 carrots, trimmed, peeled, quartered lengthwise,
   and cut into 1½-inch lengths

1 can (14.5 ounces) beef broth

1 small tomato, cored, peeled, seeded,
   and chopped

3 fresh parsley sprigs

2 bay leaves

¾ teaspoon salt

½ teaspoon dried thyme

¼ teaspoon black pepper

6 ounces white mushrooms *or* cremini
   mushrooms, stems removed and caps
   quartered into wedges

2 tablespoons balsamic vinegar

Chopped fresh parsley, for garnish

In a Dutch oven or large saucepan, heat 2 tablespoons of the butter and the oil. Add the onions and sauté over low heat until very tender and golden, about 30 minutes. Add the garlic and sauté 2 minutes. Remove onion mixture to a bowl.

Working in batches to avoid crowding, sauté the meat in Dutch oven until browned, about 10 minutes per batch, adding more oil as needed. As meat browns, add to onion mixture in bowl.

To Dutch oven, add a little of the beer, scraping up any browned bits from bottom of pan. Return onion mixture and meat to pan. Add the carrots, the remaining beer, and enough of the beef broth to just barely cover meat and vegetables. Add the tomato, parsley sprigs, bay leaves, salt, thyme, and pepper. Bring to a boil. Lower heat and simmer, partially covered, until meat is very tender, about 1¼ hours. Uncover occasionally to skim foam from top, and stir.

Add the quartered mushroom caps to stew. Simmer, partially covered, another 30 to 45 minutes or until mushrooms are tender and meat is very tender.

Remove the bay leaves and discard. Using a large slotted spoon, remove about 1½ cups of onion and carrots from stew and place in food processor. Puree. Stir back into stew. For thicker consistency, puree more onion and carrots.

Stir in the vinegar and simmer 10 minutes. Ladle stew into shallow soup bowls. Garnish with chopped parsley, and serve.

serving tip: Mashed potatoes, boiled potatoes, or wide egg noodles make the perfect side dish for this stew.

47

beef

One evening in a restaurant in Hanoi, four of us had ordered a whole range of different dishes for dinner, and one choice was a beef stew. I know about beef stew—one of my first food memories is of my mother's, with chunks of potatoes and carrots. I thought that trying such a benchmark dish here might give me some insight into Vietnamese cooking. Throughout their history, the Vietnamese have incorporated into their own cuisine elements borrowed from peoples who have occupied their country, starting with the Chinese two thousand years ago. This particular dish, with its meat and carrot combination, reflects the French colonial period, which ended in the 1950s.

vietnamese spicy beef stew with carrots and star anise

(bo kho)

MAKES 6 SERVINGS

When the waiter brought our food, the stew arrived in a small clay pot. I took a taste and loved it, but I couldn't identify the seasonings. My dinner companions took spoonfuls, and then showed looks of puzzlement—was it clove, cinnamon, allspice, anise? Then we got it: star anise. The restaurant's food consultant, who was also the chef for the Danish consulate in Hanoi, was in the kitchen that evening. He came to visit our table and, after we chatted with him, he kindly wrote down the list of ingredients in his beef stew, on which I've based this recipe.

Traditionally the stew would be prepared without first searing the meat—to make the preparation faster and use less cooking energy—but here I've added that step in order to enrich the flavor. Even more flavor develops when the sugar in the fish-sauce marinade caramelizes as the meat is browned. Vietnamese cooks frequently introduce the caramel "note"—it naturally balances the salty fish sauce, which is used ubiquitously as a seasoning instead of crystallized salt.

¼ cup Vietnamese fish sauce (*nuoc mam*)*

4 teaspoons sugar

2 teaspoons curry powder

1 teaspoon Chinese five-spice powder

1 teaspoon red-pepper flakes

1 beef bottom round roast (about 2 pounds),
    cut into 1-inch cubes

2 stalks fresh lemongrass *or* 2 strips lemon zest

2 tablespoons vegetable oil, or more as needed

1 large yellow onion, finely chopped

3 cloves garlic, finely chopped

1 can (14.5 ounces) beef broth, plus enough
    water to equal 2 cups

4 pieces star anise

1 cinnamon stick, broken in half

5 carrots, peeled and sliced ¼ inch thick

*For Ingredient Sources, see page 199.

In a glass bowl, stir together the fish sauce, sugar, curry powder, five-spice powder, and red-pepper flakes. Add the beef cubes and stir to coat meat. Cover and let marinate at cool room temperature for 1 hour; stir from time to time to keep meat coated.

Trim root ends from the lemongrass. Trim off green ends, leaving 2 to 3 inches of the white portion. Slice in half lengthwise and reserve.

In a large saucepan or Dutch oven, heat the oil over medium-high heat. Working in batches to avoid crowding the pot, add beef and brown on all sides, about 15 to 20 minutes total. As it browns, remove meat to a plate. Adjust heat so bottom of pan doesn't get too dark.

Add the onion and garlic to pan, adding more oil as needed to prevent sticking. Add a little of the beef broth, scraping up any browned bits from bottom of pan. Cook until onion begins to soften, 5 to 10 minutes.

Return meat to pan, and add remaining beef broth, the star anise, cinnamon stick, lemongrass, and any remaining marinade. Simmer, partially covered, until meat starts to become very tender, about 2 hours. Make sure the stew simmers gently and does not boil.

Add the carrots and cook until they are tender and meat is very tender, about another 30 minutes. Fish out the star anise, cinnamon stick, and lemongrass and discard them. Serve the stew hot.

serving tip: Serve the stew as is, or over cooked rice noodles, jasmine rice, or plain white rice.

In Indonesia there is a dish called *rendang,* in which cubes of water buffalo meat or beef are slowly cooked in coconut milk until the milk is reduced to its oil and the sauce becomes very thick. The result is that the meat is almost preserved and can be kept without refrigeration for a while. I once heard about an Indonesian student studying in the U.S. who, after a vacation holiday in Indonesia, brought back with him coffee cans full of *rendang* to have as a treat.

indonesian spicy beef in coconut sauce

MAKES 4 SERVINGS

In this recipe, the coconut milk is not cooked to the point where it becomes oil, but rather remains a thick creamy sauce. The result reminds me of a Stroganoff sauce, but with a more complex interplay of flavors— surprisingly, the pungent shrimp paste and the chiles are tamed by the coconut milk. This is actually a simple dish to prepare.

2 cloves garlic, sliced

2 red chiles, cored, seeded, and sliced

1 teaspoon tamarind paste*

1 tablespoon warm water

½ teaspoon Malaysian shrimp paste
   (*petis udang*)*

1 tablespoon vegetable oil

1 small yellow onion, sliced

½ teaspoon ground ginger

1 pound boneless chuck, cut into 1-inch cubes

1 can (14 ounces) coconut milk

*For Ingredient Sources, see page 199.

In a mortar with a pestle, crush together the garlic and chiles to make a paste. In a small bowl, using your fingers, mash together the tamarind paste and warm water, removing any seeds, until the liquid is somewhat thickish and the paste is evenly distributed. Transfer to a small bowl. Stir in the shrimp paste and garlic-chile paste.

In a saucepan, heat the oil. Add the onion and sauté over medium heat until softened and lightly browned, about 6 minutes. Stir in the chile mixture along with the ginger and sauté 1 to 2 minutes. Add the beef and coconut milk. Bring to a gentle boil. Lower heat and simmer, partially covered, until beef is tender and sauce is thickened, about 1 hour. Serve.

serving tip: Since the sauce is so rich, rice is the perfect accompaniment.

In Eastern Africa, there is much archaeological evidence that seeds, such as from the pumpkin and the sunflower, have been part of the diet there for thousands of years. Pumpkin seeds, pounded or ground, are often stirred into stewlike dishes to thicken and add flavor. Here, for even more depth, I've added a range of sweet spices—cumin, coriander, allspice, cloves, and cinnamon—as well as molasses. This full-bodied combination stands up well to the pickled chile.

african beef-and-kale stew with pumpkin-seed sauce

MAKES 4 SERVINGS

A cut of beef that is ideally suited for this dish (as I learned from the butcher at New York City's Jefferson Market, where I purchase a lot of my meat) is sirloin tail, the thin strip of meat at the end of a sirloin steak. The tail is lean, with great flavor, and it cooks quickly. It's also cheaper per pound than regular sirloin. By the way, if you're not a fan of kale, you can substitute fresh spinach or just leave the kale out altogether.

1 cup pumpkin seeds

3 tablespoons vegetable oil

1 pound sirloin steak tail *or* regular sirloin,
cut into small cubes

1 medium-size yellow onion, chopped

1 small sweet red pepper, cored, seeded,
and chopped

1 pickled hot chile, cored, seeded, and chopped

1 teaspoon ground cumin

½ teaspoon ground coriander

½ teaspoon ground allspice

¼ teaspoon ground cloves

¼ teaspoon ground cinnamon

½ teaspoon salt

¼ teaspoon black pepper

1 can (14.5 ounces) beef broth

1 can (15 ounces) crushed tomatoes

2 tablespoons light molasses

1 cup loosely packed chiffonade (thin strips)
of stemmed, fresh kale

Toasted pumpkin seeds, for garnish (optional)

In a large, dry skillet, working in batches if necessary, toast the pumpkin seeds over medium heat, stirring from time to time, until lightly browned and very fragrant, 3 to 4 minutes—don't get too close to the skillet, since some of the seeds may pop. Scrape onto a plate and let cool. Place seeds in a blender or small food processor and grind very fine, but not so fine that they turn into butter.

In same skillet, heat 2 tablespoons of the oil. Working in batches if necessary to avoid crowding, add the meat and brown all over, about 4 minutes per batch. Remove browned meat to another clean plate.

To the skillet, add the remaining tablespoon oil. Add the onion, sweet red pepper, and chile and sauté until slightly softened, about 4 minutes.

Meanwhile, in a small bowl, mix together the cumin, coriander, allspice, cloves, and cinnamon. Stir the ground pumpkin seeds, spice mixture, salt, and pepper into onion mixture and cook, stirring, 1 minute. Stir in the cubes of beef, beef broth, crushed tomatoes, and molasses. Bring to a boil. Then lower heat and simmer, partially covered, until meat is tender, about 1 hour.

Stir in the kale and cook until tender, 5 to 8 minutes. Spoon stew into wide soup bowls. You can garnish the stew with toasted pumpkin seeds.

serving tips: The stew can be spooned over white rice, or can be accompanied with baked or mashed sweet potatoes, or with sautéed slices of yuca or plantains.

This recipe is an excellent example of a pot-au-feu, which literally means a "pot on the fire." Preparing a meal in a single pot over an open flame is one of the earliest cooking methods known, as evidenced by kettles dating back to the Bronze Age, about 3500 B.C. Throughout Latin America, which is home to some of our oldest cultures, there exists today a wide range of stews that are prepared in cauldrons for large gatherings.

south american beef-and-potato stew with peaches

MAKES 6 SERVINGS

They each contain many ingredients, including root vegetables, plantains, winter squashes, and a variety of meats. It may seem like a lot to handle, but there's a simple trick to cooking one of these stews, whether in a cauldron over a fire or in a pot on your own stove: just add the ingredients in the order of their cooking times and the stew will cook itself.

Frequently these stews contain fruit. I had a friend once who was dating an Argentine from Buenos Aires, and when he arrived in New York, he would often cook for us. That's when I experienced the Argentine tradition of combining meat with fruit. In my own cooking, I had often stirred dried fruits—prunes, raisins, currants, apricots, apples, pears, or cranberries—into meat or poultry dishes, and occasionally fresh apples into a favorite Normandy-style chicken-and-cream preparation. But peaches and beef were a new twist for me.

This is my adaptation of one of those complex Argentine stews that was served to me, and I've whittled down the list of ingredients to something more manageable. What I discovered from cooking this dish is that adding the fresh peaches toward the end of the cooking creates an elusive sweetness that heightens the simple richness of the meat.

2 tablespoons vegetable oil, or more as needed

1½ pounds beef chuck, cut into 1-inch pieces

1 yellow onion, chopped

2 cloves garlic, finely chopped

2 tomatoes, cored and chopped (about 1 cup)

2 tablespoons balsamic vinegar

1 teaspoon sugar

½ teaspoon dried oregano

½ teaspoon dried thyme

1 bay leaf

½ teaspoon salt

1 can (14.5 ounces) chicken broth, plus
    1 can water

1 pound Yukon Gold *or* other boiling potatoes,
    peeled and sliced

½ pound sweet potatoes, peeled, halved
    lengthwise, and sliced crosswise

3 peaches, halved, pitted, and cut into
    ¾-inch-wide wedges, *or* 1 can (15 ounces)
    peach halves, drained and cut into wedges

Chopped cilantro, for garnish (optional)

In a large pot, heat the oil. Add the beef, working in batches if necessary to avoid crowding pot, and brown on all sides, about 15 minutes. As it browns, remove meat to a plate.

Add the onion to pot, adding more oil if needed to prevent sticking, and sauté until softened, about 8 minutes. Add the garlic and sauté 1 minute. Add the tomatoes and sauté 1 minute. Add the vinegar, sugar, oregano, thyme, bay leaf, salt, chicken broth and water, and beef. Cover pot and bring to a boil. Lower heat and simmer, covered, until meat is tender, about 1½ hours, stirring from time to time.

Add the white potatoes and sweet potatoes and simmer, covered, about 20 minutes or until tender. Add more water if needed to keep ingredients covered. Add the peaches and simmer, covered, 15 minutes (or less if using canned peaches) or until peaches are tender and vegetables are very tender.

Using a slotted spoon, remove meat, potatoes, and peaches to a large platter. Ladle some of the cooking liquid over top. Serve the remaining broth in bowls as a first course or as a side dish. Garnish the meat and potatoes with chopped cilantro, if you like.

beef

pork & lamb

Quinoa (pronounced KEEN-wa), an ancient grain from the Andes, is a nutritional powerhouse because it provides a remarkable amount of high-quality protein, with essential amino acids. Probably for this reason,

pork and quinoa stew with chiles

MAKE 8 SERVINGS

and the fact that the grain survives in inhospitable environments, quinoa was one of the three food staples—the other two being corn and potatoes—that allowed the Incas to flourish in Peru for centuries before the arrival of the Spanish in the 1500s.

If you've never cooked with quinoa, you may be startled at how it expands and absorbs liquid. In this rather spicy stew, just one cup nearly explodes to fill the whole pot. For a brothier finished dish, reduce the amount of quinoa to a half cup. My liking for things quite spicy has blossomed as I've gotten older, but if your tastes go in a different direction, you can decrease the "heat" here by omitting the jalapeño and reducing the amount of hot paprika to $\frac{1}{2}$ teaspoon.

There's another cultural influence in this stew in addition to the Peruvian: the marinade for the pork, which is reminiscent of the sauce made of vinegar and spices known as *adobo* in Spanish cooking (see page xiii).

pork and marinade

3 cloves garlic

2 teaspoons salt

$\frac{1}{2}$ teaspoon black pepper

$\frac{1}{2}$ teaspoon ground cumin

$\frac{1}{4}$ teaspoon ground cloves

1 tablespoon red-wine vinegar

2 pounds lean pork, from loin or shoulder,
  cut into 2-inch cubes

stew

$\frac{1}{2}$ cup hot water

1 dried chipotle chile

1 fresh jalapeño chile, cored, seeded,
  and chopped

3 tablespoons vegetable oil

1 teaspoon hot paprika

$\frac{1}{8}$ teaspoon turmeric

2 yellow onions, finely chopped

1 sweet red pepper, cored, seeded, and chopped

1 clove garlic, finely chopped

1 teaspoon salt

1 can (14.5 ounces) chicken broth, plus enough
  water to equal 4 cups

1 cup quinoa

3 tablespoons chopped fresh cilantro, for garnish

pork and marinade: In a mortar with a pestle, or with the side of a chef's knife on a cutting board, crush together the garlic, salt, pepper, cumin, and cloves to make a paste. Transfer to a large bowl and stir in the vinegar. Add the pork. Cover and refrigerate 3 hours or overnight.

stew: In the $\frac{1}{2}$ cup hot water in a small bowl, soak the dried chipotle 15 minutes. Core and seed chipotle, then chop it. Process chipotle, its soaking liquid, and the jalapeño in blender or small food processor.

In a large skillet, heat 2 tablespoons oil and the paprika and turmeric, about 1 minute. Working in batches, add the pork and sauté over high heat until browned, about 5 minutes per batch. Remove pieces to a plate as they brown. Add the onion and sweet red pepper to skillet and sauté, scraping up browned bits from bottom, until softened, about 8 minutes. Stir in garlic and sauté 1 minute. Stir in chile mixture and cook until liquid has evaporated, about 3 minutes. Stir in the salt.

Scrape mixture into a large saucepan. Stir in the broth and water mixture and bring to a boil. Stir in the pork. Cover pan. Gently simmer until pork is tender, about $1\frac{1}{2}$ hours, stirring from time to time.

Meanwhile, toast quinoa: In a large skillet, heat remaining 1 tablespoon oil. Add quinoa and cook, stirring occasionally, just until it begins to lightly color, about 3 minutes. Scrape onto a large plate.

When pork is tender, stir in toasted quinoa. Cover and simmer until quinoa has expanded, germ ring is visible, and grains are tender, 10 to 15 minutes. To serve, sprinkle with cilantro.

serving tip: Leftovers are easily reheated, but if the stew is too dry (because the quinoa has expanded), you may need to add a little liquid, either water or chicken broth.

home cooking

It had been cold and drizzly all day as we explored the winding streets of the Old Quarter in Hanoi. One of my traveling companions was a Thai who owns a *benjarong* china shop in Bangkok and is quite skillful in the Asian art of bargaining. I watched with admiration as he stood in the narrow street in front of a stall offering some good-quality Vietnamese lacquerware, and bargained for twenty minutes with the owner. Both were armed with pocket calculators, rapidly figuring exchange rates from Thai *baht* to Vietnamese *dong* to American dollars. It was street theater at its best.

vietnamese
braised pork in coconut

(thit kho tau)

MAKES 4 SERVINGS

Evening was approaching, and we were cold and hungry. Before leaving New York on our trip, I had heard about a restaurant called Diva, set among a row of cafés across from Hanoi's grand French-style Metropole Hotel. We headed there. When we walked in, we hesitated for a moment—the interior could have been any trendy restaurant in any American city—but the food smells were encouraging. What we discovered on the menu were some updates of Vietnamese classics, including pork simmered in coconut juice. We ordered a sampling of dishes and were not disappointed, proving that a well-conceived restaurant menu can sometimes offer a glimpse into the home cooking of a region.

This is my version—with a little help from the restaurant's chef—of the braised pork we had that evening. The dish illustrates several characteristics of Vietnamese cooking: the use of shallots rather than the yellow onion with which Americans are more familiar; the introduction of caramel flavoring to balance the saltiness of fish sauce; cooking with coconut juice (not to be confused with coconut milk); and garnishing with hard-cooked egg (another trait of South American cooking, as a way to introduce extra protein).

pork & lamb

2 tablespoons sugar

3 tablespoons cold water

1 can (14 ounces) coconut juice*

3 tablespoons Vietnamese fish sauce
   (*nuoc mam*)*

1½ pounds pork shoulder, with some fat,
   cut into 1-inch cubes

4 shallots, thinly sliced

2 tablespoons chopped fresh ginger

½ teaspoon Chinese five-spice powder

¼ teaspoon black pepper

4 hard-cooked eggs, peeled and cut into wedges

*For Ingredient Sources, see page 199.

In a clay pot or large saucepan, stir together the sugar and water. Over low heat, cook until it's a golden color, 5 to 10 minutes; watch closely, since as soon as the color begins to change, the sugar mixture can darken very quickly and burn. Remove from heat. Carefully stir in the coconut juice and fish sauce—there may be a little spattering. Return to very low heat and stir until well blended, scraping up any caramelized pieces stuck to bottom of pan.

Stir in the pork. Then stir in the shallots, ginger, and five-spice powder. Simmer, partially covered, until pork is very tender, about 2 hours, stirring from time to time and checking to make sure liquid is not simmering too hard. When done, stir in the pepper.

To serve, bring the clay pot to the table and serve from that, or spoon the stew into bowls. Garnish with the wedges of hard-cooked egg.

serving tip: For a more substantial meal, serve the stew over cooked rice noodles or white rice.

I was sitting in a café in Prague, chatting as best I could with three Czech graduate students in economics, whose English was much better than my nonexistent Czech. We were talking about politics, but not loudly, since it was July 1969 and there was intense paranoia about the Russians—well founded, it turned out, since a month later they entered the city again, as they had done the year before. Besides the conversation, I do remember, surprisingly, the simple stew I was lingering over, with its rich gravy and hint of caraway. I was told the broth had been thickened with rye-bread crumbs, and I thought, "How novel." I never forgot that stew; a food memory often endures when it is part of a charged moment.

short-rib stew with potatoes and carrots in rye bread— gingersnap gravy

MAKES 4 SERVINGS

Ten years later, as I became more involved with cooking and food as a livelihood, I discovered similar stews with German and Jewish roots in the cuisines of Eastern Europe, where the cooking liquid is thickened with rye-bread crumbs or crushed gingersnap cookies. This technique, rather than using the more familiar flour, makes for a lighter and more flavorful gravy. For this book, I've taken the memory of that Prague café's stew and worked with it, using short ribs rather than stew beef, and for a slightly Asian note, I've added star anise, creating a sweetly aromatic flavor.

To see how other cultures approach a basic beef stew, take a look at Vietnamese Spicy Beef Stew with Carrots and Star Anise (page 48), Flemish Carbonnade with Carrots (page 46), and African Beef-and-Kale Stew with Pumpkin-Seed Sauce (page 53). While the main ingredients are frequently the same from one part of the world to another, a dish's seasonings are what usually link it to a particular place or region.

pork & lamb

1 tablespoon vegetable oil

2 pounds short ribs of beef, cut into 2-inch
    lengths, with bone

3 large yellow onions, halved and sliced
    crosswise

8 whole cloves

4 pieces star anise

1¼ teaspoons salt

3 strips lemon zest

2 bay leaves

4 cups cold water

1 pound small red potatoes, with skins,
    halved or quartered

1½ pounds carrots, trimmed, peeled, and
    sliced ¼ inch thick

1 slice rye bread

¼ cup crushed gingersnaps (4 or 5 cookies)

2 tablespoons drained capers

1 to 2 teaspoons fresh lemon juice

¼ teaspoon black pepper

Chopped fresh parsley, for garnish

In a Dutch oven or casserole, heat the oil. Working in batches if necessary to avoid crowding the pan, add the ribs and brown on all sides, about 4 minutes per batch. As ribs brown, remove to a plate.

Add the onions to pot and sauté until softened, about 10 minutes. Tie the cloves and star anise in a piece of cheesecloth. Add to pot along with ½ teaspoon salt, the lemon zest, bay leaves, and water. Bring to a boil. Lower heat, partially cover, and simmer 1¼ hours, stirring from time to time.

Add the potatoes and carrots and cook another 45 minutes or until vegetables are tender and meat is very tender, and practically falling off the bone.

Tear the bread into pieces. In a food processor or blender, pulse until bread is finely crumbed. Add the gingersnap crumbs and pulse to combine.

Remove pot from heat. Using a slotted spoon, remove the solids from pot to a serving platter and keep warm. Discard the bay leaves and cheesecloth bag.

Stir bread crumb mixture into liquid in pot. Let stand until crumbs soften and thicken gravy, about 5 minutes. Whisk vigorously to blend. Stir in the capers, lemon juice, remaining ¾ teaspoon salt, and the pepper. Pour gravy into a sauceboat. Garnish the ribs and vegetables with the chopped parsley, and serve.

make-ahead tip: The ribs, with the vegetables, and the gravy can be refrigerated, separately, for up to 4 days, or frozen for up to 1 month. Reheat the ribs and vegetables in some of the gravy in a saucepan, covered, over medium-low heat. Reheat the extra gravy and serve on the side.

home cooking

Vindaloo curries are reputed to be among the most fiery of all curries, attributable to the generous use of chiles. They are a specialty along the southwest coast of India, and especially in the tiny state of Goa, underscoring the fact that the cooking of southern India tends to be "hotter" and spicier than that of the north. However, there is some speculation that initially the vindaloo seasonings were basically garlic, wine, vinegar, and a range of spices—but no chiles—resulting in a sharp taste probably similar to the Philippine *adobo,* a pork stew also flavored with vinegar and spices (see page xiii).

pork vindaloo

MAKES 6 SERVINGS

An Indian state since 1987, Goa was colonized by the Portuguese in the sixteenth century, and its capital was one of the richest cities in the world because of the spice trade between India and Western Europe. In Goa, the Portuguese introduced chiles and also pork, a meat that would never become part of the Muslim diet but was popular among the Christians and Hindus, who found ways to cook the meat with Indian seasonings.

The flavors in this dish are pleasingly complex. I've included a recipe for the vindaloo seasoning so that you can make it yourself, or you can purchase a jar of the paste already made (see Ingredient Sources, page 199). Traditionally, if made from scratch, the spices would have been roasted to mellow and enrich the flavors. I've omitted that step here, but you can easily combine the mustard seeds, cumin, cardamom, and cloves and lightly "toast" them in a dry skillet over medium heat. Let your nose be the guide for when the mixture is ready. The three sweet spices—cumin, cardamom, and cloves—are the perfect counterpoint to the fiery chiles. In addition, since hogs are now bred very lean, the moist method of cooking helps prevent the pork from drying out. Lamb, beef, shrimp, or even chicken can be substituted—but adjust the cooking times.

vindaloo seasoning

¼ cup white-wine vinegar

2 tablespoons olive oil

6 cloves garlic

3 tablespoons chopped fresh ginger

2 fresh red chiles, cored and seeded

2 teaspoons brown mustard seeds

2 teaspoons ground cumin

½ teaspoon ground cardamom

¼ teaspoon ground cloves

pork

2 pounds pork loin, cut into 1-inch pieces

2 tablespoons olive oil, or more if needed

2 medium-size yellow onions, finely chopped

1 cup chopped, peeled tomatoes *or* 1 can
    (14.5 ounces) diced tomatoes, undrained

1 cinnamon stick

2 tablespoons chopped fresh cilantro (optional)

vindaloo seasoning: In a blender or small food processor, combine all the ingredients for the seasoning mixture. Process until smooth.

pork: In a large bowl, combine the Vindaloo Seasoning and the pork, tossing to coat pork well. Cover bowl and refrigerate for 2 to 6 hours.

In a large skillet, heat the oil over medium-high heat. Working in batches if necessary to avoid crowding skillet, add the pork to skillet and sauté until lightly browned, about 4 minutes. As pork browns, remove it to a plate. Add the onions to skillet and sauté until lightly golden and softened, about 10 minutes, adding more oil if needed to prevent sticking. Return pork to skillet, and add the tomato and cinnamon stick. Cover skillet and simmer, stirring occasionally, until pork is cooked through and tender, about 20 minutes. Remove cinnamon stick. Stir in the cilantro, if using, and serve.

serving tip: Accompany with cooked basmati rice or plain white rice, and spinach sautéed with garlic in oil.

First, let me explain briefly what celery root is, in case you haven't encountered it before. There are two kinds of cultivated celery. Most people are familiar with the green stalks, but not with celeriac (which is also known as celery root). Celeriac has an enlarged root about the size of a turnip, with a very rough and knobby skin. It's not a new ingredient. Alan Davidson points out in *The Oxford Companion to Food* that botanical writers were making reference to the root in the 1500s. Its texture is crunchy—a cross between a radish and a potato—and its flavor is subtly celery-like, with earthy overtones.

potato-and-celery-root gratin with prosciutto

MAKES 6 SERVINGS

Throughout Europe, celeriac is commonly used in everyday cooking, showing up in soups and stews and, for a slightly more unexpected twist, grated raw into salads. This recipe pairs celeriac with thinly sliced potatoes in a scalloped casserole, rich with heavy cream and shredded Gruyère cheese. And hidden in the center, in its own layer, is finely diced prosciutto, which adds flavor to the salt-absorbing potatoes and celeriac. For another recipe using celeriac, see Baked Knockwurst with Barley and Pears (page 75).

1 clove garlic, peeled and halved

2 teaspoons unsalted butter, at room
    temperature

1¼ cups heavy cream

¾ cup milk

1½ pounds boiling potatoes, peeled and cut
    into 1/16-inch-thick slices

¾ pound celery root, peeled and cut into
    1/16-inch-thick slices

2 to 4 ounces ⅛-inch-thick slices prosciutto,
    cut into very small dice

1 cup plus 2 tablespoons shredded Gruyère
    cheese (about 6 ounces)

Heat oven to 475 degrees. Rub the inside of a 9½ × 1½-inch glass pie dish with the garlic, and reserve garlic. Then butter the dish.

In a small saucepan, combine 1 cup of the cream and the milk and garlic and bring to a simmer. Arrange half of the potato slices and half of the celery root slices in an alternating pattern in prepared baking dish. Scatter the prosciutto and 1 cup of the cheese over the top. Repeat layering with potato and celery root slices. Slowly pour hot cream mixture over potato mixture in pie dish. Drizzle remaining ¼ cup cream over top. Sprinkle with remaining 2 tablespoons cheese.

Bake in 475-degree oven until top is lightly browned, about 15 minutes. Lower oven temperature to 375 degrees. Bake until potatoes are knife-tender, liquid has been absorbed, and top is evenly browned, about another 50 minutes. Let stand 10 minutes, then serve.

serving tip: Offer this on its own as a main dish, with a green salad and a glass of Alsatian Pinot Blanc.

In the late 1970s I traveled through Alsace with some eating buddies exploring the myriad ways of eating foie gras. About a month or two before we went there, I purposely lost some weight and stepped up my exercise program, but I'm not sure it helped. Besides learning everything I ever wanted to know about goose liver on that trip, I also experienced firsthand lots and lots of choucroute—the classic Alsatian casserole with sauerkraut, sausages, and smoked meats.

alsatian smoked pork chops with sauerkraut and apples

MAKES 4 SERVINGS

What follows here is a pared-down choucroute, made with smoked pork chops (requiring only reheating) and store-bought sauerkraut. If you live in a neighborhood where you can find a pork butcher, you're lucky, because he'll probably have some excellent-quality sauerkraut. If no such luck, then stick with the plastic-bag variety you'll find in most supermarket refrigerator cases. I doctor it up with some potato to add body, apple for sweetness, cider for a little more edge, and juniper berries for a very subtle background taste.

pork & lamb

3 tablespoons vegetable oil

$\frac{1}{2}$ pound thick-sliced bacon, cut into
very small squares

2 yellow onions, halved and sliced crosswise

2 cloves garlic, finely chopped

2 pounds refrigerated prepared sauerkraut,
rinsed

2 small Granny Smith apples, peeled, cored,
and grated

1 boiling potato, peeled and grated

1 cup chicken broth

$\frac{1}{2}$ cup apple cider

$\frac{1}{2}$ teaspoon dried thyme

1 bay leaf

6 juniper berries

3 whole cloves

2 pounds smoked pork chops, $\frac{1}{2}$ to $\frac{3}{4}$ inch thick

In a Dutch oven or casserole, heat the oil over medium heat. Add the bacon and sauté until browned, about 8 minutes. Using a slotted spoon, remove bacon to a plate. Add the onions to the pot and sauté until softened, about 6 minutes. Add the garlic and sauté 1 minute. Add the sauerkraut, grated apples, and grated potato and sauté 2 minutes. Add the chicken broth, cider, thyme, bay leaf, juniper berries, and cloves. Bring to a simmer and cook, covered, 30 minutes.

Tuck the pork chops and the bacon into sauerkraut mixture. Cover pot and simmer until chops are heated through, about 30 minutes. Serve.

serving tip: Accompany with boiled potatoes and a variety of mustards and pickles.

This simple, almost bland-looking dish in shades of white and beige is characteristic of much of the home cooking of Northern and Eastern Europe, where long winters and short summers dictate which ingredients reach the dinner table. Hardy root vegetables are what survive, and pork and other meats play a large role in the cuisines of the region. Seasonings are comparatively tame. Onions and garlic are used for flavoring, and dill and caraway seem to be at the top of the list of herbs and spices.

baked knockwurst with barley and pears

MAKES 6 SERVINGS

More often than not, fruit is cooked rather than eaten fresh. This dish is almost a primer for some of the common ingredients in Northern European cooking: onion, celery root (see page 71), pears, barley, caraway, and dill.

Although there is none of the interplay of textures and flavors that one finds in the home cooking of Southeast Asia, there is a simple richness about the food in these parts of Europe that is quite satisfying.

1 tablespoon unsalted butter

1 tablespoon vegetable oil

1 large yellow onion, diced

1 small celery root (about 3/4 pound), peeled
    and finely diced (about 3 cups)

1 cup pearl barley

1 can (14.5 ounces) beef broth

Cold water, as needed

1 pound knockwurst (skin can be removed),
    sliced in half lengthwise and sliced crosswise
    1/4 inch thick

2 firm-ripe pears, stemmed, peeled, quartered,
    cored, and cut into large dice

2 teaspoons caraway seeds, crushed

3/4 teaspoon salt

1/4 teaspoon black pepper

3/4 cup chopped fresh dill, for garnish (optional)

Heat oven to 325 degrees. In a Dutch oven or casserole, heat the butter and oil. Add the onion and celery root and sauté until slightly softened, 5 to 6 minutes. Stir in the barley. Pour in the beef broth. Cover and bring to a boil.

Bake in 325-degree oven 20 minutes. If barley looks dry, add a little cold water. Stir in the knockwurst, diced pears, caraway seeds, salt, and pepper. Cover and bake another 20 minutes or until barley is tender and almost all the liquid is absorbed. Garnish with chopped dill, if desired, and serve.

serving tips: Select an assortment of mild mustards to go with this, and prepare a strongly flavored salad of shredded greens, such as romaine or endive, tossed with a citrus vinaigrette. Leftovers can be gently reheated in a covered saucepan—add a little beef broth or water if the mixture seems too dry.

I developed this recipe for an Easter issue of *Family Circle* magazine about fifteen years ago. The assignment was to come up with a recipe using ham without baking a whole one in the traditional fashion.

ham-and-lima-bean pie with cornmeal crust

MAKES 8 SERVINGS

Where to start? Why not the American South, which is famous for its high-quality hams. Pigs were for a long time essential to Southern life, providing all the obvious edible parts, including hams, ribs, bacon, knuckles, and feet (and also such by-products as lard, tallow, and hide). So I took a look at old Southern recipes that started with cooked ham, and I discovered that many dishes called for lima beans and cornmeal. That was my cue—the inspiration for this ham-and-lima-bean dinner.

The pie's cornmeal crust is one of my favorites. Here, it is made with all butter, although traditionally lard would have been used. The addition of cornmeal adds a touch of natural sweetness as well as texture, and the green part of the scallion sneaks in just the right oniony counterpoint.

Although putting together this recipe takes a little work, different parts of it can be done ahead. The finished pie is very much worth the effort, proving that some good things just take time.

78

filling

¼ cup (½ stick) unsalted butter

½ cup chopped scallions, white part only (about
    4 or 5 scallions; save green part for crust)

3 medium-size carrots, peeled, halved
    lengthwise, and thinly sliced crosswise

1 stalk celery, halved lengthwise and thinly sliced
    crosswise

½ cup all-purpose flour

2 teaspoons dried thyme

1 teaspoon ground allspice

¼ teaspoon black pepper

1 cup beef broth

1 cup heavy cream

2 to 4 tablespoons bourbon (optional)

2 cups diced (¼ inch) cooked ham
    (scant ¾ pound)

1 package (10 ounces) frozen baby lima beans,
    thawed

crust

2 cups all-purpose flour

1 cup yellow cornmeal

¼ teaspoon salt

½ cup chopped scallions, green part only
    (about 4 or 5 scallions)

1 cup (2 sticks) unsalted butter, cut into pieces

6 to 8 tablespoons cold water

Milk, for glaze

filling: In a large saucepan, heat the butter. Add the white part of the scallions, the carrot, and celery and sauté 1 minute. Cover pan and cook until almost tender, 6 minutes. Stir in flour, thyme, allspice, and pepper and cook, stirring, 2 minutes. Stir in broth, cream, and bourbon, if using, and simmer, stirring occasionally, 5 minutes or until thickened. Remove from heat. Stir in ham and lima beans.

crust: Heat oven to 425 degrees. In a bowl, mix flour, cornmeal, and salt. Stir in green part of scallions. Using pastry blender or 2 knives, cut in butter until mixture is crumbly. Sprinkle water over mixture, tossing with a fork until dough comes together. Divide in half.

Roll out half the dough on floured surface with floured rolling pin into 14-inch circle. Fit into 10-inch (2-quart) deep-dish glass pie plate. Form stand-up edge and crimp. Prick bottom of crust with fork. Line with foil, including crimped edge. Fill with dried beans.

Bake in 425-degree oven for 8 minutes. Remove foil. Bake 4 minutes. Remove to a wire rack. Lower oven temperature to 400 degrees.

Roll out the remaining dough on a lightly floured surface into a 12-inch circle. Cut into ¾-inch wide strips. Spoon ham filling into crust. Form lattice on top with dough strips, pinching strips to side of crust. Brush crust and lattice with the milk. Place on a baking sheet.

Bake in 400-degree oven 30 minutes or until crust is browned and filling is bubbly. If crust browns too quickly, cover edges with foil. Let stand 15 minutes, then serve.

serving tip: Accent with a spinach salad with red onion and oranges.

make-ahead tip: The filling and dough can be prepared a day ahead and refrigerated separately, covered.

79

As with many soups or other one-pot dishes that have their historical origins in the everyday kitchen, the variations are almost infinite, depending on the cook, the available ingredients, and the economic and social circumstances of the family. Recipes tell you much more than just about the food and how it tastes. Notice the seasonings in the soup: cinnamon and allspice. These were among the spices the Portuguese began to bring back to Western Europe in the 1500s after they opened trade routes to the Indonesian Spice Islands, bypassing the spice markets of Venice and thus ending the centuries-old monopoly created by the Venetian merchant princes.

portuguese chickpea soup with chorizo and kale

MAKES 8 SERVINGS

Inspiration for this soup-stew comes from a version of it that used to be served at Cookies, a restaurant at the very end of Cape Cod in Provincetown, Massachusetts—a town that was once home to many Portuguese fishermen. Cookies was a small place serving good Portuguese food year-round. Big windows in the front of the restaurant looked out onto Commercial Street—Provincetown's "Main Street"—and the wooden booths were a great place to sit on a bitter-cold winter afternoon, nursing a bowl of kale soup while quietly reading. There's still a restaurant on the spot, but with different owners, a different name, and a different menu.

Here are some alternatives for this recipe: Instead of the chorizo, you can use linguica—or prosciutto, which would give it a more Italian flavor. The kale adds body, but the soup-stew is fine without it. In fact, you can choose any vegetables that appeal to you if they seem to go together. But for this quantity, keep the total amount of vegetables to about a pound. And don't forget the cheese—it brings all the flavors together.

pork & lamb

4 ounces slab bacon, cut into small dice

½ pound yellow onions, chopped

4 cloves garlic, peeled

1 teaspoon ground cinnamon

½ teaspoon ground allspice

½ teaspoon salt

4 ounces chorizo links, thinly sliced

3 medium-size carrots, trimmed, peeled, and thinly sliced (halve the carrots lengthwise first, if thick)

1 sweet green pepper, cored, seeded, and chopped

¼ pound fresh kale, stemmed and torn into small pieces

1 can (14.5 ounces) chicken broth, plus water to equal 4 cups

2 cans (15 ounces each) chickpeas, drained and rinsed

Shredded Asiago, Parmesan, or Romano cheese, for topping

In a large saucepan, sauté the bacon over medium heat until fat is rendered out but bacon is not crisp, about 4 minutes. And the onions and sauté until softened and lightly golden, about 10 minutes. Add the garlic and stir in the cinnamon, allspice, and salt. Sauté until fragrant, about 1 minute. Stir in the chorizo, carrots, green pepper, and kale.

Add the chicken broth with water to the saucepan. Bring to a boil. Lower the heat and simmer, partially covered, until all the vegetables are tender, about 30 minutes.

Stir the chickpeas into the pan and heat through, about 10 minutes. Sprinkle each serving with cheese, to taste.

One of the first foods that East Coast American Indians shared with the newly arrived Europeans in the seventeenth century was hominy (dried and hulled corn kernels). A few centuries earlier, corn had been introduced to the Spanish by Native South American peoples, and the process of drying corn for hominy is related to a natural freeze-drying method that the pre-Incas in the Andes had developed even earlier for their *papas secas* (dried potatoes). Corn is not something to be taken for granted. In fact, it shows up in various recipes throughout this book, used in several different forms—in whole kernels, on the cob, as cornmeal, and as hominy. Hominy can also be ground into grits—coarse, medium, or fine-textured (see Very Rich Baked Fontina Cheese Grits with Mushrooms, page 146).

Canned hominy is fine for this casserole—just be sure to rinse it well. Its mild, distinctive taste is a good background note for the more assertive flavors of the sun-dried tomatoes and dried herbs. The leftovers reheat very well.

southern-style sausage casserole with hominy

MAKES 4 SERVINGS

pork & lamb

1 pound Italian sausage, sweet *or* hot *or*
    a combination of both

$1/4$ cup cold water

1 large yellow onion, chopped

2 cloves garlic, chopped

1 can (14.5 ounces) peeled whole tomatoes,
    with their juice

$1/2$ cup sun-dried tomatoes, packed in oil,
    finely chopped

$1/2$ teaspoon dried oregano

$1/2$ teaspoon dried thyme

$1/4$ teaspoon fennel seeds, crushed

$1/4$ teaspoon black pepper

2 cans (15 or 16 ounces each) hominy, drained
    and rinsed

$1 1/2$ cups shredded Monterey Jack cheese
    (about 6 ounces)

With a fork, pierce each sausage a couple of times. In a large skillet, combine sausage and the water. Bring water to a boil. Cover skillet, and lower heat and simmer 5 minutes. Remove sausage to paper towels. Empty skillet and wipe out with a paper towel.

Cut sausages into $1/2$-inch-thick slices. Return to skillet and sauté until browned, about 5 minutes. Using a slotted spoon, remove to paper towels.

To fat in skillet, add the onion and sauté until slightly softened, about 3 minutes. Add the garlic and sauté until fragrant, about 1 minute. Return sausage to skillet, and add the tomatoes and their juice, sun-dried tomatoes, oregano, thyme, fennel seeds, and pepper. Bring to a boil, breaking up the tomatoes. Lower heat and simmer, uncovered, stirring occasionally, until thickened, about 30 minutes.

Heat oven to 350 degrees. Add hominy to skillet and stir. Scrape half the mixture into an $11 \times 7 \times 2$-inch baking dish or other 2-quart dish. Sprinkle with $1/2$ cup of the cheese. Top with remaining hominy mixture. Bake in 350-degree oven until heated through, about 15 minutes. Sprinkle with remaining cheese. Bake until cheese on top is melted, 6 to 8 minutes. Let stand 10 minutes, then serve.

serving tip: This casserole benefits from something crisp on the side—a salad with crunchy lettuce such as romaine or a green, leafy iceberg; or lightly cooked carrots; or steamed green beans that retain a slight snap.

I love to travel to unusual, out-of-the-way places. Newfoundland had always been high on my list, and when I started talking seriously about visiting that distant Canadian province, my partner, Tom—a man who always went out of his way to humor me—agreed to tag along.

french-canadian sausage-and-apple pie with cheddar

MAKES 8 SERVINGS

Fishing is one of the major sports in Newfoundland, and while neither of us fished, we did love to eat fish, and there we had some of the best cod ever. Oddly enough, the most memorable dish I discovered on that trip was a sausage pie. I found it in a small French restaurant on the tiny island of Saint Pierre, a French protectorate just south of Newfoundland and accessible by ferry through often very rough waters. The seas were so high, in fact, that our return from Saint Pierre was delayed by a day. This gave us a chance to explore the restaurants, which was how I ran across that version of *tourtière,* a well-seasoned pork pie traditionally served in Quebec as part of a Christmas Eve buffet. (The English meat pies are in the same family.)

A few days later we spent a night in a small guest house in a fishing village up the coast from Saint John's, Newfoundland's capital, and for the evening meal we were served yet another delicious pork pie. I thought that was strange for an oceanside village, even though we also had the usual cod dishes.

In the recipe that follows, I've added apples for a little sweetness, and I soon discovered that this pie is equally delicious whether it is served warm or at room temperature, or as leftovers straight from the refrigerator. A savory pie with a flaky crust has always been, for me, one of the most satisfying meals.

85

pork & lamb

crust

1 recipe Pastry, (page 9; omit pecans) *or*
    1 ready-to-use, refrigerated, folded pie crust

filling

1 pound sweet Italian sausage

¼ cup plus ⅓ cup apple juice

4 tablespoons (½ stick) unsalted butter

3 tart apples, such as Granny Smith, peeled,
    quartered, cored, sliced, and tossed in bowl
    with squeeze of lemon juice

2 teaspoons brown sugar

¼ teaspoon ground cinnamon

⅛ teaspoon ground allspice

⅛ teaspoon ground mace

2 medium-size Vidalia onions *or* other
    sweet onions, coarsely chopped

2 cloves garlic, finely chopped

1 egg, lightly beaten

2 tablespoons chopped fresh parsley

1¾ cups shredded sharp cheddar cheese
    (about 7 ounces)

1 teaspoon fresh lemon juice

¼ teaspoon salt

¼ teaspoon black pepper

crust: Preheat oven to 400 degrees. Line a 9-inch pie plate with the pastry, cover with foil, and fill with dried beans or rice. Bake in 400-degree oven 10 minutes. Remove foil. Prick pastry with fork if it has bubbled up in spots. Bake until golden, 10 to 15 minutes more. Remove to wire rack to cool. Leave oven at 400 degrees.

filling: Prick the sausages with a fork. Place in single layer in large skillet. Add the ¼ cup apple juice and enough cold water to come to a depth of ¼ inch. Gently boil, turning sausages once, until liquid evaporates, 8 to 10 minutes. Continue to cook until fat is rendered, 2 to 3 minutes. Remove to paper towels to drain. Wipe out skillet.

In the skillet, heat 2 tablespoons of the butter. Add the apples, brown sugar, cinnamon, allspice, and mace and sauté until apples just begin to soften, 4 to 6 minutes. Transfer to a bowl.

Heat remaining butter in skillet. Add onions and sauté until golden, 10 minutes. Add garlic and cook until fragrant, 1 minute. Add remaining ⅓ cup apple juice and cook, scraping up bits from bottom, until liquid is slightly reduced, 1 minute. Add to apples in bowl.

Remove casings from sausages. Crumble into bowl with apples. Add egg, parsley, all but ½ cup cheese, lemon juice, salt, and pepper. Spoon into the crust. Sprinkle with remaining cheese. Place on a baking sheet.

Bake in 400-degree oven until top begins to brown, 10 to 15 minutes. Lower to 375 degrees. Bake until browned and bubbly, 15 to 20 minutes more. Let stand 10 minutes, then cut into wedges and serve.

serving tip: For a side dish, try blanched rounds of zucchini and yellow squash, dressed with a mustardy vinaigrette.

home cooking

I'm not sure this dish would win prizes for its appearance, although it is a wonderful study in browns and beige. The recipe comes from a good friend of mine, Dui Seid, a Chinese-American conceptual artist

chinese braised lamb with chestnuts, mushrooms, and red dates

MAKES 4 SERVINGS

and sometime traveling companion. He recently re-created the dish from his childhood memories of it, and with a little help from his mother. She lives in the New York City borough of Queens, which has an extraordinary number of ethnically diverse neighborhoods.

You will have to do a little shopping before making this stew, since it calls for a number of Chinese dried ingredients; or you can obtain them from mail-order sources. The complex flavor of the finished dish is very satisfying and warming, with its sweet, earthy, meaty overtones—an Asian cousin of European osso buco and other simmered dinners.

8 ounces dried chestnuts*

12 pieces dried red dates*

Cold water

16 dried bean sticks* *or* threads, broken into
    5- to 7-inch lengths

20 dried whole black mushrooms*

1 tablespoon vegetable oil

2 pounds lamb shanks *or* lamb neck

3 cloves garlic, chopped

2 teaspoons chopped, peeled fresh ginger

2 tablespoons soy sauce

1 tablespoon sliced, peeled fresh ginger

⅓ cup cold water

4 teaspoons cornstarch

½ teaspoon salt

¼ teaspoon black pepper

*For Ingredient Sources, see page 199.

In a medium-size bowl, place the dried chestnuts and dates in 3 cups of water. Place the bean sticks in another bowl and cover with water. Place the mushrooms in a third bowl and cover with water. Let everything soak overnight. Drain them all, reserving their soaking liquids. Strain mushroom liquid through a sieve lined with a double layer of dampened paper towels to remove any grit.

In a large pot, heat the oil. Add the lamb and sauté until browned all over, about 15 minutes. As it browns, remove lamb to a plate. Add the garlic and chopped ginger to pot and sauté 1 minute or until fragrant. Stir in the soy sauce. Return lamb to pot and stir to coat.

Measure soaking liquid from chestnuts and dates, and add soaking liquid from mushrooms and bean sticks as needed to equal 3 cups. Add to lamb in pot. Bring to a boil, then lower heat and simmer, partially covered, for 1 hour, stirring occasionally.

Skim fat from surface. Add the sliced ginger, chestnuts, dates, mushrooms, and bean sticks to pot. Simmer, partially covered, until meat and other ingredients are very tender, about another 1 hour, occasionally uncovering and stirring. Using a slotted spoon, remove solids from liquid to a platter, separating chestnuts, dates, mushrooms, bean sticks, and lamb.

In a small bowl, stir together the ⅓ cup cold water and cornstarch until well blended and smooth. Stir in 1 cup of hot liquid from pot. Stir cornstarch mixture into pot and gently heat, stirring, until gravy thickens, about 2 minutes. Season with the salt and pepper. Pour the gravy into a sauceboat. Serve platter of lamb with its accompaniments, with the gravy on the side.

serving tip: A mound of hot white rice is a welcome side dish.

pork & lamb

As its name suggests, this casserole is traditionally made with mutton or lamb. You can substitute ground beef for the lamb, but the resulting dish, according to some, would more properly be called a cottage pie.

shepherd's pie with garlic-horseradish-potato topping

MAKES 6 SERVINGS

"Hidden" in this recipe are two additional recipes. The first is a simple one for roasted garlic, which on its own can be spread over toasted bread or croutons, or mixed with cooked vegetables. The second is for mashed potatoes—flavored with horseradish and the roasted garlic, and enriched with heavy cream and butter—which makes a very tasty side dish.

When you shop for ground lamb, don't go looking for it on a Monday—at least not first thing in the morning. Butchers and supermarket meat departments usually get fresh deliveries of meat on Monday morning, and it's not until later in the afternoon that they'll have the trimmings for ground lamb.

roasted garlic

1 whole head garlic

2 tablespoons olive oil

mashed potatoes

3 pounds Yukon Gold potatoes *or* red-skin
    potatoes, with skins, quartered

$1^1/_2$ teaspoons salt

$^1/_4$ cup ($^1/_2$ stick) unsalted butter, cut into pieces

$^1/_2$ cup heavy cream

$^1/_4$ cup milk

1 egg

2 tablespoons bottled horseradish, drained

$^1/_4$ teaspoon black pepper

filling

2 tablespoons olive oil

2 yellow onions, chopped

2 cloves garlic, chopped

1 pound ground lamb

1 teaspoon dried thyme

1 teaspoon dried rosemary

$^1/_2$ teaspoon salt

$^1/_4$ teaspoon black pepper

1 tablespoon all-purpose flour

1 cup canned chicken broth

1 package (10 ounces) frozen green peas,
    thawed

roasted garlic: Heat oven to 300 degrees. Separate the cloves of garlic from the whole head. Discard papery skins, but leave cloves unpeeled. Place in shallow baking dish. Drizzle with the olive oil and toss to coat garlic well. Bake in 300-degree oven until softened, about 45 minutes. Let cool. Cut off hard end of each clove and squeeze soft pulp into small bowl.

mashed potatoes: While garlic is roasting, place the potatoes in a large saucepan with enough cold water to cover by 1 inch. Add 1 teaspoon of the salt. Bring water to a boil, and cook potatoes 15 minutes or until tender. Drain. Return potatoes to pan. Add the butter, cream, milk, egg, horseradish, remaining $^1/_2$ teaspoon salt, the pepper, and roasted garlic. Mash until fluffy.

filling: While potatoes are cooking, heat the oil in a large skillet. Add the onions and sauté until very soft, 10 to 15 minutes. Add the garlic and sauté 1 minute. Remove to a plate. Add the lamb to skillet and sauté, breaking up clumps with a wooden spoon, until lightly browned, 4 to 6 minutes. Carefully pour off any excess liquid. Stir in the thyme, rosemary, salt, pepper, onion mixture, and flour and cook 1 minute. Stir in the chicken broth. Bring to a boil. Lower heat and simmer, covered, 5 minutes. Stir in the peas.

Increase oven temperature to 375 degrees. Spoon filling into a $13 \times 9 \times 2$-inch glass baking dish. Spread mashed potatoes evenly over filling, swirling the top decoratively. Bake in 375-degree oven 40 minutes or until topping is lightly golden and filling is bubbly. Let stand on a wire rack for 15 minutes, then serve.

serving tip: A green salad that includes very thin slices of fennel bulb makes a crisp counterpoint to this rich casserole.

pork & lamb

In rural Africa, meat is not commonly found in the diet, and when it does make an appearance in a dish, it is usually for a festive occasion or some special event. Goat and lamb are more frequently used for cooking than is beef, and the toughness of the meat requires long simmering.

south african lamb-and-green-bean stew

MAKES 4 SERVINGS

This meat-and-potato stew is based on a South African dish called *bredie,* which contains chunks of vegetables such as squash, pumpkin, and beans—in this case, green beans. For a lamb stew, the seasonings here might be considered exotic: chiles and ginger, and papaya, which contributes a sweet-tartness. That combination of flavors has its origins in South Africa's strategic location. During the sixteenth and seventeenth centuries, as the Portuguese, Dutch, and English sailed back and forth between Europe and the Spice Islands of Indonesia, they used the southern tip of Africa as a staging point for taking on fresh food and other provisions. Over time they established settlements. As historian Charles Corn points out in his book *The Scents of Eden: A History of the Spice Trade,* nutmeg, mace, cloves, cinnamon, and pepper drove the world economy four hundred years ago in much the same way as oil does today. What occurred in South Africa was the cross-fertilization of cultures, as Europeans introduced the spices of the East Indies and certain European food preferences.

In this recipe, I use small pieces of lamb shoulder and neck on the bone. When prepackaged in a market, this combination is usually called "lamb stew meat." I like the shoulder cut because it tends to be fatty, adding more flavor to the stew—the bone helps, too. The shoulder is a tougher cut, needing longer simmering, which means even more development of flavor.

92

2 tablespoons vegetable oil, or more as needed

1½ pounds lamb shoulder stew meat, with bone

2 small yellow onions, coarsely chopped

3 cloves garlic, finely chopped

2 tablespoons finely chopped, peeled fresh ginger

½ cup cold water

1 pound green beans, trimmed and cut into 1-inch lengths

2 medium-size boiling potatoes, peeled and cut into ½-inch cubes

2 fresh serrano chiles, cored, seeded, and chopped

1 teaspoon salt

½ teaspoon dried thyme

¼ teaspoon black pepper

1 papaya, halved, seeded, peeled, and cut into ½-inch cubes

In a large, heavy skillet, heat the oil over medium heat. Working in batches if needed to avoid crowding the skillet, add the lamb and sauté until browned, about 20 minutes total. As pieces brown, transfer them to a plate. Add the onion to skillet and sauté until softened, about 8 minutes, adding a little more oil if needed to prevent sticking. Add the garlic and sauté 1 minute.

Return meat to skillet, and add the ginger. Cover skillet tightly with a sheet of aluminum foil and a lid on top of that. Cook over very low heat for 30 minutes. Stir lamb occasionally and check to make sure it is not browning too quickly.

Stir the water, green beans, cubes of potato, chiles, salt, thyme, and pepper into the skillet. (If this is too much quantity for the skillet, transfer to a large saucepan or Dutch oven.) Bring to a boil. Cover skillet tightly, lower heat, and simmer, occasionally uncovering and stirring, until meat and vegetables are tender, about 1 hour. For the last 15 minutes of simmering, gently stir in the cubes of papaya. Serve.

serving tip: Warm pita bread or other flat breads, stacked in a basket, is a good choice for soaking up the flavorful juices.

pork & lamb

This is a dish from South Africa called *bobotie*, made with curried ground lamb, bread soaked in milk, almonds, raisins, and bay leaves—lots of them. It's a kind of a flat meatloaf. Often made with leftover cooked lamb or beef, chopped fine, it can also be prepared with fresh ground lamb (as it is here), or ground beef.

south african curried lamb casserole with raisins and almonds

MAKES 6 SERVINGS

South African cuisine is described by some as the collision of the Dutch and Malayan pantries. The roots of this dish can be traced to the mutton or lamb curries of Malaya and Indonesia, which became popular in the South African colonial outposts established there by Dutch traders. The spices such as cardamom, coriander, cumin, and turmeric that were ground and blended to give these curries much of their characteristic flavor came from the Spice Islands (the Dutch East Indies). The eye-watering "heat" component derives from the chile brought from the New World by the Portuguese, and subsequently used by the Spanish, Dutch, Malays, and Indians in their own cooking.

Comparing the curries of Thailand with those of the Malayan-influenced Dutch underscores one of my premises—that the biggest differences in cooking are frequently based on what you have in your spice cabinet. The red and green curries of Thailand are fiery with chiles and tempered with coconut milk, whereas in this recipe the taste is less fiery, and raisins and chutney add a softening sweetness, which appeals more to the European palate.

94

2 pounds very lean ground lamb

2 slices white bread

1 cup milk

3 tablespoons unsalted butter

2 yellow onions, coarsely chopped

2 cloves garlic, finely chopped

2 tablespoons curry powder

1/2 cup dark seedless raisins

2 tablespoons slivered almonds

2 tablespoons fresh lemon juice

1 tablespoon mango chutney, large pieces
    chopped

1/2 teaspoon salt

1/4 teaspoon black pepper

2 eggs

6 bay leaves

In a large skillet, sauté the ground lamb, working in batches if necessary to avoid crowding the skillet, until lamb is no longer pink, 3 to 4 minutes per batch. As it browns, remove lamb to a colander to drain excess water and fat.

In a small bowl, soak the bread in 1/4 cup milk for 20 minutes, turning it over occasionally. Squeeze excess milk out of bread and then tear it into pieces.

Heat oven to 375 degrees. Lightly butter a 13 × 9 × 2-inch glass baking dish. In a large skillet, heat the butter. Add the onions and sauté until softened, 5 to 8 minutes. Add the garlic and curry powder and sauté 1 minute. Remove from heat.

In a large bowl, mix together the lamb, onion mixture, raisins, almonds, lemon juice, chutney, salt, pepper, and 1 egg, slightly beaten, until all ingredients are evenly distributed. Spoon into prepared baking dish. Tuck the bay leaves into lamb mixture.

Bake in 375-degree oven 30 minutes. In a glass measuring cup, stir together the remaining egg and remaining 3/4 cup milk. Pour over lamb mixture. Bake until egg mixture is set, 10 to 15 minutes. Remove and discard bay leaves, then serve.

serving tip: Try this with a shredded carrot salad on the side.

pork & lamb

seafood

Here is a simple Swedish casserole, in the tradition of a peasanty potato gratin, where combining just a few ingredients results in a very rich taste. Imagine scalloped potatoes with a golden brown, crunchy crust assertively flavored with anchovies, and you will understand why it's called "Temptation."

jansson's temptation

MAKES 6 SERVINGS

The culinary origins of this dish are hazy, but there is one story that seems to be retold the most often. Some time long ago, a very devout Swede named Erik Janson was forbidden by his church to indulge in anything enjoyable. But occasionally he managed to sneak this delicious potato gratin onto his table to steal a few moments of pleasure. Why and how the spelling of Janson changed is a historical mystery.

1 cup heavy cream

¾ cup milk

1 teaspoon fennel seeds, crushed

2 small tins (about 2 ounces each) salted
   flat anchovy fillets

2 pounds Yukon Gold potatoes *or* other
   boiling potatoes, with skins, sliced
   ¹⁄₁₆ to ⅛ inch thick

1 pound Vidalia onions *or* other sweet onions,
   thinly sliced and separated into rings

¼ teaspoon white pepper

Fresh dill, for garnish (optional)

Heat oven to 475 degrees. In a small saucepan, combine the cream, milk, and fennel seeds. Bring to a gentle boil. Remove from heat and let steep while preparing the anchovies, potatoes, and onions.

Remove individual anchovy fillets to paper towels to drain and reserve the oil in the tins. Dip a paper towel into a little of the anchovy oil and grease bottom and sides of a 13 × 9 × 2-inch baking dish. In the dish, layer ingredients as follows: one-third of the potato slices, half the onions, half the anchovies, half the white pepper; then one-third of the potato slices, the remaining onions, the remaining anchovies, the remaining white pepper; and finally the remaining potatoes. Drizzle reserved anchovy oil over top of casserole.

Pour cream mixture into a 2-cup measuring cup. Slowly drizzle over top of potatoes, stirring fennel seeds up from bottom of measuring cup so they are evenly distributed.

Bake in 475-degree oven until top begins to brown, 15 to 20 minutes. Lower oven temperature to 375 degrees. Continue to bake until top is golden brown and crisp, potatoes are fork-tender, and most of cream mixture has been absorbed, about another hour. If top begins to get too brown, tent loosely with foil. Let casserole stand 10 minutes. Serve, garnished with fresh dill, if you like.

serving tips: Accompany this gratin with a plain green salad, such as romaine, perhaps with a little watercress, dressed in a balsamic vinaigrette. Leftovers of the gratin can be eaten cold or at room temperature, or they can be reheated in a microwave oven, a 350-degree oven, or under the broiler.

Many years ago, I was traveling with a friend west along the French Riviera at a fast clip on our motorcycles. Our destination was Spain's Costa Brava. We had been warned that the Spanish motorcycle policemen seemed to be always looking for the easy buck, and to be careful—Franco was still alive and running Spain. So I was not surprised when, not long after we had crossed the border into Spain's Catalan region, two of

catalan baked fish with potatoes and parsley

MAKES 4 SERVINGS

them pulled me over, even though I hadn't been speeding. At that point, my traveling partner was far ahead of me. I figured out that the policemen— quite elegant in their tailored uniforms and peaked hats—wanted my passport, and the rest I could easily guess: Once the document left my hand, I would have to pay to get it back. Well, I screamed something about the American consulate and that I wasn't going to move from that spot and I wasn't handing over anything. They got the message: I wasn't worth the effort. They climbed back on their bikes and left.

I was relieved but badly shaken, and was happy to see my traveling companion coming back for me. To recover from my near disaster, we quickly found a roadside restaurant and tossed down several glasses of red wine. We ordered dinner, and what I remember most is a delicious fish dish with potatoes, tomatoes, and herbs, which I later learned was a classic home-style Catalan preparation. Having grown up in New England, I knew about potatoes in clam and fish chowders, but I had never eaten fish baked on a bed of thinly sliced potatoes. It was wonderful. The potatoes were perfectly tender, and richly flavored with the herbed juices from the fish and the tomatoes and the most perfumy olive oil I had ever tasted.

101

potato layer

1 pound Yukon Gold potatoes, peeled and
    sliced $\frac{1}{8}$ inch thick

Extra-virgin olive oil

4 cloves garlic, finely chopped

4 scallions, trimmed and thinly sliced

$\frac{1}{2}$ teaspoon salt

$\frac{1}{4}$ teaspoon black pepper

fish layer

1 to $1\frac{1}{4}$ pounds 1-inch-thick halibut, tuna, *or*
    other firm-flesh fish steaks

2 tomatoes, cored and cut into thin wedges

$\frac{1}{4}$ teaspoon dried rosemary

$\frac{1}{4}$ teaspoon dried thyme

2 tablespoons finely chopped parsley

$\frac{1}{2}$ teaspoon salt

$\frac{1}{4}$ teaspoon pepper

2 tablespoons extra-virgin olive oil, or more
    if you like

1 large lemon, halved

potato layer: In a large pot of boiling water, cook the potatoes until slightly tender, about 4 minutes. Drain well in a colander, and then rinse under cold running water to stop the cooking. Transfer to paper towels and gently blot dry.

Heat the oven to 400 degrees. Lightly coat inside of an 8 × 8 × 2-inch baking dish with the olive oil. Layer sliced potatoes in the dish, sprinkling layers with the garlic, scallions, salt, and pepper.

fish layer: Arrange the fish on top of the potatoes. Place the tomato wedges around outside edge of casserole. Sprinkle fish and potatoes with the rosemary, thyme, parsley, salt, and pepper. Sprinkle fish and tomatoes lightly with the olive oil, then squeeze the lemon halves over the casserole.

Bake in 400-degree oven until fish begins to flake and potatoes are tender, 15 to 25 minutes.

make-ahead tip: The potatoes, fish, and tomatoes can be assembled in the baking dish a few hours ahead. Cover tightly with plastic wrap and refrigerate. Let the casserole come to room temperature before baking or, if taking it directly from refrigerator to oven, allow a little extra baking time.

The cooking technique called for in this recipe is used in most cuisines—we in the West call it sautéing and in some cases pan-searing, and in Asian cuisines it's called stir-frying. It works for practically any food: meat, fish, poultry, and vegetables. The trick is to keep the pieces small and uniform in size so everything cooks quickly and at the same rate. An added bonus is that if you add a little liquid at the end of the cooking, you can quickly reduce it to concentrate flavors and produce a pan sauce.

pan-seared sea bass with crispy ginger threads

MAKES 4 SERVINGS

When I first started cooking for myself, a friend gave me a bunch of rusted cast-iron skillets, which I cleaned up and seasoned with cooking oil and coarse salt. That's when I learned how to sauté. A black peppercorn–encrusted chop steak with a brandy-cream sauce was the first recipe I attempted, and it still remains in my repertoire some twenty-five years later. One lesson I learned that first time around was that cast iron will discolor a cream sauce, so choose your pan wisely.

I have to watch my cholesterol level, so the fish recipe here is healthier for me than that beefsteak—but not by much, since it includes a brown butter sauce. There's a double hit of ginger: the grated fresh ginger in the sauce, and crispy threads for a garnish. The ginger is deliciously accented by a splash of orange juice.

I like using sea bass in this dish because it has a firm texture that holds up well to the high heat, and its flavor is pleasingly rich. Cod, haddock, or halibut would work too.

ginger threads

1 piece fresh ginger (2 × 1 inch), peeled

2 teaspoons vegetable oil

sea bass

1 tablespoon vegetable oil

4 sea bass fillets *or* other firm white fish
   (about 4 ounces each, 1 inch thick), with skin

½ teaspoon salt

⅛ teaspoon white pepper

2 tablespoons unsalted butter

1 teaspoon grated, peeled fresh ginger

1 tablespoon orange juice

ginger threads: Cut the piece of ginger lengthwise into very thin slices. Stack slices and cut lengthwise into very thin strips—you're creating threads of ginger. In a large nonstick skillet, heat the 2 teaspoons oil over medium heat. Add ginger threads and sauté, stirring often, until brown and crisp, 3 to 4 minutes. Transfer to paper towels to drain. Wipe out skillet with a paper towel.

sea bass: In the same skillet, heat the 1 tablespoon oil over medium-high heat. Season the fillets with the salt and white pepper. Place them skin side down in skillet. Lower heat slightly and cook until skin is browned and crisp, about 3 minutes. Turn fillets over, lower heat to medium, and brown other side, about 3 minutes. Add the butter and grated ginger. Cook until fillets are opaque in center, about another 4 minutes. As the fillets cook, turn them over once or twice and baste with the pan sauce. Transfer fillets to a platter.

Stir the orange juice into skillet and cook 30 seconds. Drizzle over fillets, garnish with the crispy ginger threads, and serve.

serving tips: I've accompanied this with roasted baby beets—carrots would also be good—and very thinly sliced pan-fried potatoes. Other alternatives are garlic mashed potatoes, orzo, or white rice, with steamed Chinese long beans or regular green beans.

Bali was "re-discovered" by Western travelers in the 1930s, and since then it has gradually become more and more popular as a tourist destination; an international airport opened there in 1969. Remarkably, though, there is still a sleepiness about the island, with its terraced rice patties and cloud-ringed mountains. Rice is grown everywhere on the island, and fish is prominent in Bali's cuisine, as one might expect, despite a mythical fear of the oceans and the evil spirits that are said to reside there. The fresh waters in the interior also provide a variety of fish.

balinese
fried fish with *sambal*

(ikan goreng)

MAKES 4 SERVINGS

Balinese cooking is distinguished by the generous use of chiles, as is much of the regional cooking of Indonesia. In this dish, the fish is coated with both turmeric (imparting a bright yellow color), and rice flour, which adds a subtle crunchiness when the fish is fried.

What adds another dimension to this fried fish is *sambal,* a spicy chile condiment popular throughout southern India, Indonesia, and Malaysia. Each home cook perfects his or her own *sambal.* They can be purchased ready-made, but like curry powders, the best are those made from scratch. For this recipe, it's worth searching out the lemongrass, shrimp paste, and tamarind paste to achieve the balance of sweet and sour that goes so well with the slightly sharp, almost mustardy-tasting turmeric coating on the fish (see Ingredient Sources, page 199). The shrimp paste I've used here is *petis udang* from Malaysia—it's very dark and very thick, with a slightly sweet taste. Frying it with other ingredients for the *sambal* helps to temper its flavor. Even without the *sambal,* this fish dish is delicious.

107

1 tablespoon rice flour *or* all-purpose flour
   or fine yellow cornmeal

1 teaspoon turmeric

1/2 teaspoon salt

4 fillets red snapper *or* sea bass (about
   1 pound total)

Juice of 1 large lime

sambal

2 tablespoons tamarind paste* (see Note, below)

6 tablespoons warm water

2 small cloves garlic, sliced

2 small hot red chiles, cored, seeded, and sliced

2 tablespoons vegetable oil

1 stalk lemongrass, trimmed, tender portion
   cut into 1-inch pieces and crushed with
   side of knife

1 teaspoon Malaysian shrimp paste
   (*petis udang*)*

1 teaspoon brown sugar

Vegetable oil, for frying fish

Note: You may substitute 3 tablespoons tamarind
concentrate for the tamarind paste and warm water.

*For Ingredient Sources, see page 199.

On a piece of waxed paper, mix together the rice flour, turmeric, and salt. Rub the fish fillets with the lime juice. Coat fillets on all sides with flour mixture. Refrigerate 30 minutes.

sambal: In a small cup, combine the tamarind paste and warm water. Mash paste into water with your fingertips, removing any seeds, until liquid is thickish and pulp is evenly distributed. In a mortar with a pestle, crush together the garlic and red chiles to make a paste. In a small skillet, heat the oil over medium heat. Add the garlic-chile paste and the lemongrass and stir-fry 1 minute. Add the shrimp paste and stir-fry 30 seconds. Add the tamarind mixture and sugar and stir-fry until sauce thickens, about 1 minute. Spoon *sambal* into small bowl and let come to room temperature. Then remove pieces of lemongrass, scraping off any *sambal* mixture, and discard the lemongrass.

Into a large skillet with straight sides, pour enough vegetable oil to reach a depth of about 1 inch. Heat oil until it reaches 365 degrees on a deep-fat frying thermometer. Using a slotted spatula, slip fillets into hot oil. If necessary, fry in two batches to avoid crowding skillet. Fry until brown and crusty on bottom, about 3 minutes. Carefully turn fillets over and fry until brown and crusty, about another 3 minutes. (Cooking time will vary, depending on thickness of fish.) Using slotted spatula, remove fillets to paper towels to drain. Transfer to a platter and serve with *sambal* on the side.

Drawn or clarified butter is the classic "sauce" for dipping and slathering warm pieces of steamed or boiled lobster. But what follows here is a butterless alternative that accents lobster equally well. Taught to me by a friend from Thailand, the sauce is an amazing blend of hot, sour, and salty tastes. In a Thai kitchen, fish sauce would usually be added to provide the saltiness; but in order to enhance and not overpower the delicate flavor of lobster, this recipe substitutes salted water—and what better pairing for something from the sea?

steamed lobster with thai hot sauce

MAKES 4 SERVINGS

The amount of chiles in this recipe may seem like it's too much—and in fact the sauce is an eyebrow raiser—but the pepper "heat" is balanced by the garlic and lime juice.

thai hot sauce

¼ cup cold water

1 teaspoon salt

10 cloves garlic, chopped

10 small red hot chiles, stemmed and
thinly sliced (for a milder sauce, remove
the seeds and membranes)

¼ cup lime juice (2 to 3 limes), or to taste

4 live select lobsters (about 1½ pounds each)

thai hot sauce: In a small saucepan, bring the water to a boil. Stir in the salt until dissolved. Remove from heat. In a mortar with a pestle, crush together the garlic and chiles until they form a paste. Stir in the lime juice to taste, working the liquid into the paste. Stir in 3 tablespoons of the salted water and blend well. Taste. If necessary, adjust the balance between hot, sour, and salty. The sauce can also be made in a small food processor or blender. Divide the sauce among 4 small cups and serve as a dipping sauce with the lobster.

lobsters: Steaming whole lobsters cooks them more slowly than boiling, thus reducing the chance of overcooking. Figure on about a 5-gallon pot for steaming the lobsters. If the pot is smaller, cook lobsters in two batches. Rig pot with a steamer, or in lieu of that, a metal colander turned upside down. Pour in about an inch or two of sea water, or tap water with about 2 tablespoons salt added. If you can't find anything in your kitchen that will work as a steamer, you can do without. Cover pot and bring water to a boil.

Take the live lobsters, and if the claws are secured with rubber bands, snip bands off with kitchen shears. Be careful. Once one claw is "unleashed," it will move in the direction of your hand as you remove the band from the other claw—but you can move faster than the lobster. Place live lobsters headfirst into steamer rack or directly into boiling water in bottom of pot. Cover and steam for about 14 minutes. When done, the shells will be bright orange-red, tail curled, and antennae easily pulled out.

Using tongs, remove lobsters. Using a clean kitchen towel to protect your hands, break off the knuckles and claws, and cut off the tail. The tail meat should be creamy white, and any roe or eggs should be bright orange-red and solid. Serve with Thai Hot Sauce for dipping.

home cooking

110

Several years ago for a couple of summers in a row, I would spend a few weeks in a house rented from friends of mine in Maine on their small island in Penobscot Bay. Penobscot Bay and the small fishing village of Stonington at the end of Deer Isle, not far from the island where I stayed, have now achieved culinary fame, since New York City restaurants have started "importing" scallops, mussels, and other seafood from the

maine
lobster chowder
with bacon and potatoes

MAKES 4 SERVINGS

region. The island I was on is a barred island, which means at low tide you can get to it in a four-wheel-drive vehicle by navigating some tricky sandbars, and at high tide you use the outboard. Living was pretty simple. No electricity—both the stove and the refrigerator ran off propane. My friends were on good terms with the local lobsterman, and as a result, two wooden crates floating at the end of the dock were always full of live lobsters.

It was in that island house that I developed this recipe. To make it, you begin with whole live lobsters, because you want the shells to make the richly flavored and slightly sharp lobster broth. Allow enough preparation time so the chowder can "mature" in the refrigerator for an hour. And the final flavor? The potatoes and bacon as well as the lobster are subtly accented by the "sweetness" of the cumin and paprika. There's something very satisfying about all these flavors together—one spoonful just makes me quietly moan. We all have at least one dish in our flavor memories that makes us react that way.

111

seafood

2 live select lobsters (about 1½ pounds each)

2 bay leaves

1 carrot, sliced

1 small yellow onion, chopped

1 stalk celery, sliced

2 strips of bacon, chopped

2 teaspoons unsalted butter

1 cup chopped scallions (about 9 scallions)

1 teaspoon Hungarian sweet paprika

½ teaspoon ground cumin

1 pound all-purpose potatoes, peeled and
    cut into ¼-inch cubes

1 cup heavy cream or half-and-half

¼ teaspoon salt

¼ teaspoon white pepper

2 cups corn kernels (from 4 ears fresh corn)
    or frozen, thawed

Thinly sliced scallion greens or snipped
    fresh chives, for garnish

In a large covered pot, steam the lobsters in 2 inches of boiling water for about 12 minutes or until shells are bright red, tail is curled, and antennae are easily pulled out (see Steamed Lobster with Thai Hot Sauce, page 109, for more tips on steaming). When cool enough to handle, remove the meat from the claws, knuckles, and tails; cut into large pieces. Refrigerate the meat. Split open the body, and remove the head sacs and discard. Remove all or most of the green tomalleys. Place carcasses and shells in a pot and cover with 2 to 3 quarts of cold water. Add the bay leaves, carrot, onion, and celery. Bring to a boil. Lower heat and simmer, uncovered, for 1 hour. Strain and discard solids; you should have about 4 cups of broth.

In a large saucepan or Dutch oven, sauté the bacon until fat is rendered. Add the butter to pot and heat. Add the scallions and sauté until softened, about 2 minutes. Stir in the paprika and cumin. Add the diced potatoes and enough lobster broth to cover them. Bring broth a boil, and cook until the potatoes are tender, 15 to 20 minutes. The liquid should be slightly thickened. You can mash the potatoes a bit for a thicker chowder, if desired.

Add the cooked lobster meat, cream, salt, and pepper. Let cool. Then refrigerate, covered, 1 hour to "mature" the flavors.

Add the corn to the pot. Gently reheat chowder. Garnish each serving with thinly sliced scallion greens or snipped fresh chives, and serve.

Late in the afternoon one July, I was reading on the deck of the house we rented from friends on their small island in Maine's Penobscot Bay. I glanced up when I heard the engine of the lobster boat approaching

baked honey-glazed mackerel

MAKES 4 SERVINGS

the shore. It was that time of day when the lobsterman checked his traps. He spotted me and started waving with a fish in his hand. I waded out and he handed me a couple of mackerel, not too long out of the water.

Back in the kitchen while cleaning the fish, I thought about how I was going to fix them. Our stove ran off bottled propane, and while the oven would hold a temperature, the burners on top didn't create a very hot flame. So I decided I would bake the fish. There was a jar of local honey in the cupboard along with some apple-pie spices, so I thought, Why not something vaguely Moroccan. It worked. The spicy heat of the allspice, cloves, and cayenne deliciously undercuts the mouth-filling sweetness of the honey. These flavorings also go well with strongly flavored bluefish, trout, tuna, and salmon.

114

½ cup honey
2 tablespoons cold water
½ teaspoon ground allspice
½ teaspoon ground cloves
¼ teaspoon cayenne pepper
1¼ pounds mackerel fillets

Heat oven to 425 degrees. In a small bowl, stir together the honey, water, allspice, cloves, and cayenne pepper. Place the fillets in a baking dish, and spread with the honey mixture.

Bake in 425-degree oven for 8 to 12 minutes, depending on the thickness of fillets, until the fish is opaque in the center and just begins to flake when prodded with a fork. Divide into 4 portions and serve.

serving tips: Orzo is a good side dish with this, or small boiled potatoes. For a vegetable, try steamed green beans.

seafood

Some of my time these days is spent on Cape Cod, in a small town called Wellfleet, where I have access to the local oysters (those Wellfleet oysters you see on restaurant menus) as well as all kinds of fish.

cape cod
clam pie

In Orleans, a few towns away at the elbow of the Cape, there is a fish market open all year round, and on a shelf in their freezer case are frozen clam pies. Often when I'm driving by and I think of it, I'll stop and pick up a couple to stash in my own freezer for an easy supper when I don't feel like cooking.

Those frozen pies are the inspiration for the recipe here. Both follow the tradition of home cooking that extends a small amount of protein into an ample number of servings, by adding lots of other delicious ingredients, especially low-cost ones.

Clam pie is found in many early American cookbooks and church and civic organization "receipt" books. But these days, one sees it less in the current clamor of get-it-on-the-table-quick kind of eating, although using canned minced clams speeds up the process a bit.

There are two ways you can handle the crust: Make the double crust as directed below, which requires a little dexterity in maneuvering the top crust; or, use all the dough to make just a top crust. If you do the latter, you need to bake it a little longer to ensure that the top crust is properly cooked through and flaky.

116

filling

4 cans (6.5 to 7.5 ounces each) minced clams
1 cup light cream
1 large yellow onion, diced
1 rib celery, diced
1 pound Yukon Gold potatoes *or* other
    boiling potatoes, peeled and diced
½ teaspoon salt
¼ teaspoon dried thyme
¼ teaspoon black pepper
2 slices thick-cut bacon

crust

1 recipe Pastry (page 9; omit pecans)

glaze

1 egg
1 teaspoon milk *or* light cream

filling: Drain clams, reserving ½ cup liquid. In saucepan, mix liquid, cream, onion, celery, potatoes, salt, thyme, and pepper. Simmer until potatoes are just tender, 10 minutes. Add clams. Remove from heat.

Heat oven to 350 degrees. In a skillet, sauté the bacon until crisp, 10 to 15 minutes. Remove to paper towels to drain. Crumble.

crust: Divide Pastry dough into a two-thirds and a one-third portion. On a floured surface, with a floured rolling pin, roll out larger one into 13-inch square. Fit into bottom and up sides of an 8 × 8 × 2-inch square metal baking pan, with crust overhanging edges of pan. Cover dough in pan with foil and fill with dried beans or rice.

Bake in 350-degree oven 15 minutes. Remove to wire rack. Remove foil with beans. Using fingers, gently press dough to close any openings. Let cool 10 minutes. Increase oven to 450 degrees.

Stir bacon into filling. Spoon filling into crust. Roll out remaining dough on floured surface into an 8 × 8-inch square for top crust.

glaze: In a small cup, stir together the egg and milk. Brush glaze over rolled-out pastry. Place pastry, glazed side down, on top of baking dish. Pinch edges of bottom and top crust together to seal. Crimp edge decoratively. Brush glaze over top crust and edges. Cut several steam vents in top crust.

Bake in 450-degree oven 10 to 15 minutes or until golden. Lower oven to 350 degrees. Bake until filling is bubbly, 20 to 25 minutes. If edges start to get too dark, cover with foil. If top browns too quickly, tent with foil. Let stand 15 minutes, then serve.

serving tip: Goes great with corn on the cob.

seafood

For some reason, even though we're not Catholic, my mother thought we should observe the fish-on-Fridays rule in our house. Sometimes she took the easy way out and served us Gorton's fish sticks—extra tartar sauce, please—and at other times it was codfish cakes, made from scratch, either with fresh cod or salt cod, the latter requiring a little extra preparation since it needed to be soaked.

codfish cakes, thai-style

MAKES 4 SERVINGS

With my increased interest in all things Asian over the last several years, I've taken those simple New England fish cakes and made them over into something Thai, accented with fresh ginger, red curry paste, and cilantro. Follow my advice and buy a small bag of rice flour for this recipe: dredging the fish cakes in rice flour results in a slightly crunchier exterior than if using all-purpose flour.

mustard sauce

¾ cup mayonnaise

2 teaspoons Dijon mustard

fish cakes

1 pound fresh cod fillets, cut into chunks

2 teaspoons grated, peeled fresh ginger

1 to 2 teaspoons bottled Thai red curry paste*

¼ cup fresh cilantro leaves

2 scallions, trimmed and chopped

1 clove garlic, chopped

1 egg

2 teaspoons light brown sugar

1½ teaspoons salt

½ cup white rice flour, for dredging

2 tablespoons vegetable oil, for frying, or more
    as needed

*For Ingredient Sources, see page 199.

mustard sauce: In a small bowl, stir together the mayonnaise and mustard. Cover and refrigerate until ready to use.

fish cakes: In a food processor, combine the cod, ginger, curry paste, cilantro, scallions, garlic, egg, brown sugar, and salt. Process until smooth. Transfer to a bowl. Form into 8 equal patties, about ¼ cup per patty. Spread the rice flour on waxed paper and coat the patties all over. Place the patties on a waxed-paper-lined baking sheet and refrigerate 30 minutes to firm the fish mixture and coating.

In a large, nonstick skillet, heat the oil. Working in batches to avoid crowding the skillet, add patties and sauté until golden brown, turning once, 3 to 4 minutes per side. Using a slotted spatula, transfer patties to paper towels to drain. Serve with the mustard sauce on the side.

serving tip: Coleslaw and/or steamed broccolini are my choices for sides. The mayonnaise-mustard sauce also makes a perky spread for sandwiches or even a topper for hot dogs and hamburgers.

seafood

Indonesian and Malaysian curries usually incorporate coconut milk to tame their fiery spiciness. Not too long ago in our culinary history, the mention of the word "coconut" would conjure up images of old Bob Hope and Bing Crosby movies, and for the slightly more advanced among us, visions of that laughing-eyed Latin woman who danced with fruit on her head. That's all changed. We've moved beyond the piña colada with its cream of coconut. We've come to understand that the coconut palm is considered the "tree of life" in Southeast Asia and India, since its coconut milk and grated coconut meat are essential ingredients in the cuisines of those regions, and the trunk, leaves, and the shell of its nut are used for everything from rope to furniture to roofing—nothing is wasted.

indonesian tuna curry

MAKES 6 SERVINGS

In this recipe, I use a commercial curry powder and punch it up with fresh ginger and turmeric. For the distinctively sour note in this curry, I use a tamarind concentrate rather than the paste that appears in other recipes in this book. I prefer the concentrate when I'm moving quickly through meal preparation. And this is a fast curry—it's ready in half an hour.

120

3 or 4 fresh green chiles *or* red chiles, cored
    and seeded

4 shallots, coarsely chopped, *or* ¼ cup chopped
    yellow onion

2 cloves garlic, chopped

1 piece fresh ginger (½-inch), peeled and sliced

1 teaspoon curry powder

1 teaspoon turmeric

1 tablespoon tamarind concentrate*

½ teaspoon salt

1 can (14 ounces) coconut milk

1 pound fresh tuna *or* mackerel, cut into
    2-inch chunks

*For Ingredient Sources, see page 199.

In a small food processor or blender, combine the chiles, shallots, garlic, ginger slices, curry powder, turmeric, tamarind concentrate, and salt. With on-and-off pulses, process mixture until finely chopped. Slowly add ½ cup of the coconut milk while blending, until mixture is well pureed. Pour into a large skillet. Stir remaining coconut milk into skillet. Simmer about 10 minutes to blend the flavors.

Add the tuna. Cover skillet and simmer 10 to 15 minutes or until tuna is cooked through.

serving tip: Serve curry with basmati or wild pecan rice.

seafood

This is another American classic that I've fiddled with, making it slightly Indian by adding a few pinches of curry powder. I ate many servings of tuna-noodle casserole while growing up, and if my memory is accurate, it was a Thursday-night dish.

curried tuna-noodle casserole with mushrooms and peas

MAKES 6 SERVINGS

The original was made with canned soup. Here I make the mushroom mixture from scratch; it really doesn't take that much time and tastes much fresher. Vary the amount of curry powder depending on the "heat" level of the kind you're using and your own taste.

8 ounces egg noodles

1 tablespoon unsalted butter

1 pound cremini, shiitake, oyster, *or* other
    mushrooms, tough stems removed, sliced
    (about 5 cups)

3/4 cup frozen peas, thawed

3/4 cup thinly sliced scallions (about 6 scallions)

1 small sweet red pepper, cored, seeded,
    and chopped

2 to 3 teaspoons curry powder

3 tablespoons all-purpose flour

1 1/4 cups milk

1/2 cup heavy cream

1/4 cup chopped flat-leaf parsley

1/2 teaspoon salt

1 can (12 ounces) solid white tuna packed
    in water, drained and broken into chunks

1/2 cup crushed cornflakes *or* butter crackers,
    for topping

Cook the noodles, following package directions. Drain and set aside.

Meanwhile, in a large nonstick skillet, heat the butter over medium heat. Add the mushrooms and sauté until softened and liquid has been released, 6 to 8 minutes. Add the peas, scallions, red pepper, and curry powder and sauté until pepper is slightly softened, about 3 minutes.

In a small bowl, whisk together the flour, milk, and cream until smooth and blended. Stir into mushroom mixture in skillet. Bring to a boil. Lower heat and simmer, stirring frequently, until thickened, about 2 minutes. Remove skillet from heat. Stir in the parsley and salt.

Heat oven to 375 degrees. Using a rubber spatula, fold the cooked noodles and the tuna into sauce in skillet. Scrape into an 8- or 9-inch square baking dish or other 2- to 2 1/2-quart baking dish. Sprinkle cornflakes or crackers over top.

Bake in 375-degree oven until casserole is bubbly and topping is toasted, about 20 minutes. Let stand 10 minutes, then serve.

serving tip: Keep the accompaniment simple: a romaine salad splashed with an orange vinaigrette.

make-ahead tip: Earlier in the day, assemble the casserole without sprinkling on the topping, and refrigerate, covered. To serve, sprinkle with the topping and bake as directed, allowing a little extra baking time since the casserole is cold.

With its touch of lime and spicy-sweet "heat" from the cloves, cardamom, and ground red pepper, this soup takes its inspiration from the Caribbean. To put the soup in a more familiar perspective, just think of the sweet-potato-and-scallop combination as mimicking the fish and potatoes in a thick and creamy New England clam chowder.

caribbean sweet potato soup with scallops

MAKES 4 SERVINGS

In the late 1970s I worked in a restaurant on Martha's Vineyard called The Black Dog, which is still there. You may have seen the T-shirts with the black Labrador retriever on them (if I remember correctly, Bill Clinton bought one of those shirts for Monica). When I was working there, it was not nearly as exciting, although we did serve a very popular clam chowder that was so thick you could stick a spoon in it and it would stand upright. Ironically, the chowder base was made by some fellow on Nantucket and then flown to the Vineyard, where we doctored it with heavy cream and a couple of other ingredients. As the orders went flying out of the kitchen, I often wondered what the soup would taste like if it were made with sweet potatoes. Years later, I began to spot just such a combination on restaurant menus in New York City and while perusing some Latin American cookbooks in preparation for a trip to the Caribbean to celebrate a friend's fiftieth birthday. So some twenty years after the thought first occurred to me, here's my variation, made with scallops rather than clams.

When I make this soup, I really don't have a preference between the heavy cream or the coconut milk; depending on my mood, either can be my favorite for the moment. I've also successfully made this soup with shrimp and crabmeat instead of scallops.

1½ pounds sweet potatoes, peeled and cubed
2 cans (14.5 ounces each) chicken broth
4 whole cloves
½ teaspoon turmeric
½ teaspoon cardamom
½ teaspoon salt
⅛ teaspoon ground red pepper
½ cup heavy cream *or* coconut milk
½ pound sea scallops, halved if large
1 tablespoon fresh lime juice
Chopped fresh cilantro, for garnish (optional)

In a large saucepan, combine the sweet potatoes, chicken broth, cloves, and turmeric and bring to a boil. Lower heat and simmer until potatoes are tender, about 15 minutes. Remove cloves.

Working in batches, puree potatoes with broth in a food processor. Return to saucepan. Stir in the cardamom, salt, red pepper, and cream or coconut milk. Bring to a simmer. Add the scallops and simmer until cooked through, about 5 minutes, being careful not to overcook them. Stir in the lime juice, garnish with the cilantro, if desired, and serve. If the soup is too thick for your taste, thin with a little chicken broth.

Cooking food in banana leaves is an easy way to retain moisture and insure against overcooking. The Balinese employ this method frequently, combining spice mixtures with poultry and fish in these little packets, which are then grilled, baked, or steamed. The French bake dishes in a similar fashion, a technique they call *en papillote,* using parchment paper to seal in juices as the food cooks.

balinese spicy shrimp packets

(pais udang)

MAKES 4 SERVINGS

During a recent trip to Indonesia, I was delighted to come across many of these banana leaf–wrapped packages, the concealed contents of which I could only imagine. The aromas, however, hinted at something mouthwatering. And I was never disappointed when I carefully unwrapped the leaves.

The original version of this shrimp dish that I sampled in Bali used *kemiri,* also called candlenuts. Since they're difficult to find in New York, and perhaps in most places in this country, I've substituted macadamia nuts. And if banana leaves are not available—check with your florist or grocer—aluminum foil works well for the packets, although the presentation is not nearly as attractive.

3 macadamia nuts

2 shallots, sliced

1 piece fresh ginger ($\frac{1}{2}$ inch), peeled and sliced

$\frac{1}{2}$ teaspoon salt

$\frac{1}{4}$ teaspoon turmeric

$\frac{1}{4}$ teaspoon sugar

1 small red chile, seeded and sliced

1 teaspoon tamarind paste*

2 tablespoons warm water

1 pound peeled and deveined medium shrimp
(leave tails on, if desired); or sea bass, cod,
or snapper fillets, cut into small pieces

4 banana leaves, blanched (page xiii) or
four 6-inch squares of aluminum foil

8 to 12 very thin slices lime

2 scallions, trimmed and diagonally sliced
into $\frac{1}{2}$-inch pieces

12 fresh mint leaves or basil leaves

*For Ingredient Sources, see page 199.

In a small food processor, coarsely grind the nuts. Add the shallots, ginger, salt, turmeric, sugar, and chile and process until they form a paste. In a small cup, using your fingertips, mash together the tamarind paste and the warm water, removing any seeds, until the liquid is brown and thickish and the pulp is evenly distributed. Add to processor and blend until smooth. Scrape into a medium-size bowl. Add the shrimp or fish and toss to coat. Let stand 15 minutes.

Heat oven to 350 degrees. Spread out the banana leaves or foil squares on a flat work surface. Divide shrimp or fish among the 4 leaves or squares. Top with lime slices, scallion, and mint or basil leaves, dividing equally. Wrap up banana leaves around filling and secure with toothpicks or tie with kitchen twine, or pleat edges of foil together, enclosing filling.

Bake on middle oven rack in 350-degree oven 15 minutes or until shrimp are cooked through. Place on dinner plates, and let each diner unwrap his or her own parcel.

serving tip: Accompany with steamed white rice or sticky rice, and with sautéed vegetables, such as a combination of spinach, corn kernels, and green beans.

seafood

Sour, sweet, bitter, and salty are the four major "tastes" by which we experience food, and they register in very specific parts of the mouth. I've included this dish because it is a good example of the family of simple stews that incorporate a sour note balanced by other flavor-absorbing ingredients. Here, the sour is white vinegar and dill pickle, and it's tempered by both the mild cod and the potatoes.

bavarian fish stew with vegetables and vinegar

MAKES 6 SERVINGS

This recipe is based on a *pichelsteiner,* a German stew that is popular in Bavaria. Usually prepared with meats such as pork, beef, or mutton, it is also delicious with a mild white fish such as cod.

Consider some of my other recipes that focus on the sour. There is the Philippine Sour Soup with Chicken (page 29), which incorporates tamarind and tomatoes for a sharp background note. Catalan Baked Fish with Potatoes and Parsley (page 101) also pairs potatoes and fish, with tomatoes and lemon contributing the acidic touch. The lime juice–based Thai dipping sauce for lobster (page 109) sharpens the sweet richness of the lobster.

An acid can also chemically cook an ingredient, as in the famous Peruvian ceviches. In this recipe, the cod "marinates" in the vinegar for thirty minutes, so it actually begins to "cook," further enhancing the tenderness of the fish at the end of the simmering.

The bacon in the stew adds a smokiness as well as the obvious saltiness that marries well with the sour. While working out this recipe, I tried throwing in some caraway seeds. The combination of vinegary sauerkraut and caraway works in Alsatian choucroute, so why not here? Well, the caraway got in the way of the other flavors and unbalanced the stew's simplicity, proving the point that *too* many flavors can "muddy" a dish.

130

2 pounds firm, white-fleshed fish fillets,
   such as cod *or* haddock
¼ cup distilled white vinegar
½ teaspoon salt
¼ teaspoon black pepper
3 slices bacon, coarsely chopped
1 yellow onion, coarsely chopped
2 carrots, trimmed, peeled, and diced
2 small leeks, trimmed, sliced, and rinsed well,
   or 6 scallions, trimmed and thinly sliced
   (about ¾ cup)
1 pound boiling potatoes, peeled and sliced
   ¼-inch thick
⅛ teaspoon ground cloves
2 cups cold water

garnishes
½ cup chopped dill pickles, or to taste
¼ cup chopped fresh parsley

Place the fish fillets in a glass baking dish. Rub both sides of fillets with the vinegar and season with the salt and pepper. Let stand in a cool place for 30 minutes.

In a 2-quart saucepan, heat the bacon over medium heat. When fat begins to render out, about 3 minutes, add the onion, carrots, leeks or scallions, and potatoes. Cover saucepan and cook vegetables until slightly softened, uncovering from time to time and stirring, about 8 minutes. Add the cloves and water and bring to a boil.

Cut the fish crosswise into 1- to 2-inch-wide strips. Lay fish on top of vegetables in the pot. Lower heat and simmer, uncovered, 15 minutes. Then cover pan, lower heat even more, and simmer for another 5 to 10 minutes or until fish is cooked through.

Spoon the fish, vegetables, and broth into deep soup bowls. To garnish, stir in the chopped pickles and sprinkle with the parsley, and then serve.

serving tip: As is often the case, a loaf of crusty bread with some softened unsalted butter would be ideal with this stew.

seafood

vegetables

I was served a portion of this moist but not soupy stew, along with many other dishes, as part of an Indian wedding feast being staged for a group of journalists I was traveling with recently. The place was Cochin, a coastal city in Kerala Province, at the southwest tip of India. We were seated at long tables in the outdoor courtyard of the Brunton Boatyard, a modern hotel built in the Portuguese manner in the Fort Cochin area. At the beginning of the feast, a huge banana leaf was laid before me on the table—this became my disposable plate. A mound of rice was spooned into the center. Next, there appeared several dollops of different *sambals,* spicy condiments containing a chile or two. And around the edge of my banana leaf, servers arranged about a dozen mounds of other dishes, including *aviyal.* I reached for a fork, but not a utensil was to be seen anywhere. The Indian woman seated next to me paused in the midst of our conversation and told me to watch her. She used the fingertips of her right hand to first mix a little bit of *sambal* into a portion of rice, and then took a smidgen of one of the other mounds and, after blending it with the rice-*sambal* mixture, neatly scooped the small pile into her mouth. I tried my best to follow her example, but at the end of the meal my banana leaf seemed to be considerably messier than hers.

indian vegetable stew with yogurt and coconut

(aviyal)

MAKES 6 SERVINGS

In this rich vegetarian stew, based on the one I had that evening, the heat of the chiles and curry powder is tempered with cooling coconut milk, a flavor combination found in much of the cooking of southeast Asia, most notably Indonesia and Thailand.

135

1 boiling potato (about ½ pound), peeled
    and cut into ½-inch cubes

2 medium-size carrots, trimmed, peeled,
    and sliced ¼ inch thick

6 ounces green beans, trimmed and cut into
    ½-inch pieces

1 small sweet potato, peeled and cut into
    ½-inch cubes

1 small sweet red pepper, cored, seeded, and
    cut into small squares

1 cup frozen peas

½ cup cold water

1 teaspoon turmeric

1 teaspoon curry powder

1 teaspoon cumin seeds, toasted

2 hot green chiles, cored, seeded, and minced

¾ cup coconut milk

¼ cup yogurt

1 teaspoon salt

1 small starfruit (carambola), thinly sliced
    or diced

In a large pot, combine the potato, carrots, green beans, sweet potato, red pepper, and frozen peas. In a 1-cup measure, stir together the water, turmeric, and curry powder. Stir into vegetable mixture. Cover and bring to a boil. Lower heat and gently cook until vegetables are tender but still retain their shape, about 30 minutes.

In a mortar with a pestle, crush the cumin seeds. Add the chiles and crush together with cumin. In a small bowl, stir together the coconut milk and yogurt. Stir in chile mixture.

When vegetables are tender, stir in coconut mixture. Gently heat through. If the stew seems a little too liquid, gently cook, uncovered, until slightly drier. Garnish each serving with slices of starfruit, or dice the starfruit and mix in.

serving tip: Serve with basmati, jasmine, or plain white rice, and an assortment of Indian flatbreads.

This strictly vegetarian dish is a satisfying combination of red lentils, corn, peas, and cauliflower, strongly seasoned with a sweet spice mixture and chipotle chiles (dried, smoked jalapeños) in *adobo* sauce (page xiii). The look and flavor of this soup are reminiscent of dishes from northern India, where lentils and cumin are often used, although the chile "heat" is more characteristic of the cooking of southern India—with an added cross-cultural note imparted by the chipotle, an ingredient from American Southwestern or Mexican cooking.

red-lentil-and-chile soup-stew with vegetables

MAKES 6 SERVINGS

This kind of soup, because it starts out meatless, can be taken in different directions with just a few simple additions. If keeping this dish vegetarian is not a concern, chicken broth can be used instead of the water, and 4 ounces of shredded cooked chicken can be added at the end of the cooking time and then gently heated through. And if you want a milder dish, a little heavy cream or coconut milk can be stirred in to temper the "heat" of the chiles.

1 small head cauliflower (about 1 pound),
    stems trimmed and separated into
    small flowerets
1 tablespoon ground cumin
2 teaspoons ground coriander
1 teaspoon ground cardamom
1 teaspoon turmeric
1 tablespoon vegetable oil
1 large yellow onion, chopped
2 cups red lentils
6 cups cold water
1 or 2 chipotle chiles in *adobo* sauce, seeded
    and chopped
½ pound plum tomatoes, cored, seeded,
    and chopped
1 cup frozen peas, thawed
1 cup frozen corn kernels, thawed
1 teaspoon salt

garnishes
2 scallions, trimmed and sliced
2 tablespoons chopped fresh cilantro

In a large saucepan of lightly salted water, cook the cauliflower flowerets until tender, about 5 minutes. Drain in a colander and rinse under cold water to stop the cooking. Set aside.

In a cup, combine the cumin, coriander, cardamom, and turmeric. In a small, heavy skillet over medium heat, toast spice mixture, stirring occasionally, until fragrant and slightly colored, about 3 minutes. Scrape into a small bowl.

In a large saucepan, heat the oil. Add the onion and sauté over low heat until tender and lightly browned, 10 to 15 minutes. Add the lentils and water. Bring to a boil. Lower heat and skim any foam from top. Stir in half the toasted spice mixture, the chipotle, and the tomatoes. Cover and gently cook until lentils are very tender, about 30 minutes.

When lentils are tender, working in batches and using a slotted spoon, remove half the lentils to a food processor. Puree. Stir back into saucepan. Stir in the peas, corn, cauliflower, salt, and remaining toasted spice mixture. (If adding shredded chicken as mentioned in the introduction to this recipe, stir it in now.) Gently heat the soup. Ladle into soup bowls, garnish each serving with the scallions and cilantro, and serve.

Peru is home to many different cuisines: Spanish, Chinese, Japanese, Incan, Italian, and African. In the mid-1990s, I was first introduced to Peru by a good friend, Anki Moromisato, a Peruvian-Japanese born in Lima and now living in New Jersey, where many Peruvians have emigrated. On several of our excursions through different neighborhoods of Lima—including the rather upscale Miraflores district with its cafés and parks, the vertical cemetery "village" at the edge of a shantytown, and an off-the-beaten-track residential neighborhood where

peruvian potatoes in cheese sauce

(papas a la huancaina)

MAKES 4 SERVINGS

Anki played volleyball late one night with old friends on lighted courts—I enjoyed this potato-and-cheese dish, a national favorite, many times. Nearly every town and cook has a different version, although the recognized origin is Huancayo, a mountain town a few hours from Lima.

I've based the version here on one I found in a twenty-year-old recipe book published in Peru, *Platos Peruanos*. Usually the cheese sauce is a vivid yellow color from the yellow Peruvian *ají* (a type of chile), and sometimes the sauce begins with cooking onion, chili powder, and turmeric together in a skillet, which enhances the Technicolor effect even more. I've kept the sauce simple—no cooking required, just mixing the ingredients in a blender. And the color in this version is a little tamer.

4 Yukon Gold potatoes, with skins

$\frac{1}{2}$ pound *queso fresco* (firmly packed
    fresh cheese) *or* fresh feta cheese *or*
    fresh farmer's cheese

$\frac{1}{2}$ cup evaporated milk

2 yellow Peruvian chiles (*aji amarillo*) *or*
    2 jalapeño chiles, cored, seeded, and
    chopped, *or* 2 teaspoons *aji* chile powder*

$\frac{1}{2}$ teaspoon salt

4 lettuce leaves

garnishes

2 hard-cooked eggs, peeled and quartered

16 pitted black olives, sliced

1 or 2 ears fresh corn, boiled, cooled, and
    cut into 1-inch sections

1 large ripe tomato, cored and cut into wedges

Parsley leaves

*For Ingredient Sources, see page 199.

In a large pot of boiling water, cook the potatoes until tender but still firm, 25 to 30 minutes. Drain and let cool.

In a blender or small food processor, combine the cheese, evaporated milk, chiles, and salt. Blend until sauce is smooth.

Peel potatoes. Slice lengthwise into $\frac{1}{4}$-inch-thick slices.

Line 4 plates with lettuce. Arrange sliced potatoes over each. Cover with cheese sauce. Garnish with the eggs, olives, corn, tomato wedges, and parsley leaves.

serving tips: Serve the potatoes at room temperature for lunch, or as an appetizer, or as a side dish with roasted meats.

The potato has been a staple for Peruvians over many thousands of years, especially in its dried form in the high Andes, and in the eighteenth century it became an essential element in Irish cuisine—yet another example of how foods migrate around the world.

irish mashed potatoes with cabbage

(colcannon)

MAKES 4 SERVINGS

The Irish created this meal-in-itself mashed-potato dish using simple ingredients: potatoes, cabbage or kale, onions, cream, and butter. In Ireland, *colcannon* was associated with Halloween, and followed in the tradition of burying charms in special holiday dishes to ensure a favorable outcome for the finder of the charm—if a tooth wasn't broken while eating it. The *colcannon* could very often be chock-full of objects: a gold marriage band, a piece of money, an old maid's thimble, and a bachelor's button—almost no room for the potatoes. Your fate could be decided for the year ahead by a biteful of this hearty dish.

143

2 pounds Yukon Gold potatoes *or* other
    boiling potatoes, unpeeled, quartered

2 cans (14.5 ounces each) chicken broth,
    plus cold water as needed

1 pound kale *or* dark green cabbage,
    stemmed (or cored), and thinly sliced

¼ cup cold water

1 pound leeks, trimmed, thinly sliced, and
    washed *or* 2 bunches scallions, trimmed,
    washed, and thinly sliced (about 2 cups)

1 cup light cream, or more as needed

3 cloves garlic, crushed

1 bay leaf

¾ teaspoon salt

¼ teaspoon ground nutmeg

¼ teaspoon pepper, preferably white

¼ cup (½ stick) unsalted butter, melted,
    plus more solid butter for garnish

In a large saucepan, mix together the potatoes, chicken broth, and enough water to cover potatoes. Bring to a boil and cook until potatoes are tender, 20 to 25 minutes.

At the same time, in another saucepan, combine the kale and ¼ cup water. Cover, bring to a boil, and cook until kale is tender, about 15 minutes. Drain, squeeze dry in paper towels, and then chop very fine.

In a third saucepan, combine the leeks, light cream, garlic, and bay leaf. The leeks should be almost covered by the cream—if not, add a little more. Cover pan and simmer until leeks are softened, 15 to 20 minutes.

Drain potatoes, reserving the cooking liquid for making soup another time. Transfer potatoes to a large bowl. Drain leeks, reserving cream and garlic, and discarding bay leaf. Add cream and garlic to potatoes and mash them together. Stir in leeks. Then stir in kale along with the salt, nutmeg, pepper, and melted butter until thoroughly blended. Bury a pat of butter in the top of each serving.

serving tips: Serve with slab bacon cooked crisply, grilled sausages, roasted chicken, duck, or goose, or all on its own. Leftovers can be shaped into small pancakes and fried in a mixture of butter and oil in a heavy skillet. Serve for lunch, breakfast, or even a snack.

My mother loves mushrooms as I do, so perhaps I've been genetically programmed to share her passion. I'm also a fan of porridges of all kinds, and in that category I include everything from oatmeal and grits to rice congee and chickpea porridge. I probably first tasted true Southern grits in my middle teens, on a family trip to South Carolina. My brother Rick was a freshman at Clemson University, and over Easter vacation that year, my parents and I drove down to visit him and his roommate and his roommate's family. Somewhere in the midst of that adventure, I remember sticking my spoon into a bowl of steaming grits and thinking, "This isn't bad." When I got older and traveled in the South on my own—college debate trips, and during spring breaks camping on beaches and playing tennis—I explored that grits memory, sampling them whenever I had the chance. And then early trips to Italy introduced me to polenta—which, I discovered, is not so very different from grits.

very rich baked fontina cheese grits with mushrooms

MAKES 6 SERVINGS

I learned over the years that you can play with the versatility of grits by taking advantage of its rich but somewhat neutral flavor. Grits are ground from hominy (dried corn kernels), so the underlying flavor has a satisfying earthiness with a touch of sweetness, much as a corn tortilla does. Building on that taste by adding one or two or three very flavorful ingredients can transform grits into something even more delicious. Like polenta, grits can be soft and very spoonable, or if baked, firm and forkable, as they are here.

For this recipe, you can mix any combination of mushrooms, following your own taste. As for the cheese, I have a special fondness for Italian Fontina and feel that it's worth seeking out a good one for that special tanginess, which matches perfectly with the mushrooms and the grits.

mushrooms

½ pound shiitake *or* other similar mushrooms,
   stemmed and cleaned

½ pound white mushrooms, stemmed
   and cleaned

1 tablespoon unsalted butter

2 teaspoons olive oil

4 leeks, trimmed, thinly sliced, and rinsed well

2 cloves garlic, finely chopped

1 teaspoon dried thyme

½ teaspoon salt

grits

5 cups cold water

1 cup grits

1 teaspoon salt

1 teaspoon unsalted butter

½ cup milk

2 eggs

½ teaspoon dried thyme

¼ teaspoon white pepper

1 cup shredded Italian Fontina cheese (4 ounces)
   or Dutch Fontina *or* Muenster cheese

mushrooms: Cut the mushroom caps in half, then cut crosswise into ⅛-inch-thick slices. In a very large skillet, heat the butter and oil over medium-high heat. Add the leeks and garlic and sauté until softened, 3 to 4 minutes. Add the mushrooms, thyme, and salt and sauté until mushrooms cook down and the mushrooms release their liquid, 5 to 7 minutes. Remove skillet from heat.

grits: In a Dutch oven or very large saucepan, bring the water to a boil. Stir in the grits and salt. Cover pan and lower heat to low. Cook, stirring occasionally, until thickened, about 20 minutes. Stir in the butter and remove from heat.

Heat oven to 350 degrees. Butter evenly an 8 × 8 × 2-inch or 11 × 7 × 1½-inch glass baking dish or a 2-quart ceramic soufflé dish.

In a small bowl, whisk together the milk, eggs, thyme, and white pepper. Stir the cheese into grits until melted. Fold in mushroom mixture. Stir in milk mixture. Spoon into prepared baking dish and spread evenly.

Bake in 350-degree oven until top is lightly browned, 50 to 60 minutes. Remove to a wire rack and let stand 15 minutes, then serve.

serving tip: This kind of richness needs crispness. Serve with cherry tomatoes, a plain green salad, or even sliced cucumbers sprinkled with cider vinegar or balsamic vinegar.

Green bean salad with roasted red peppers, green bean salad with toasted walnuts and goat cheese, plain green beans in a balsamic vinaigrette—these are just a few of the green bean salad recipes I've played with over the years. My repertoire has recently been expanded by a new addition from Southeast Asia—an Indonesian version. Indonesia is an archipelago that stretches over 17,000 islands covering a distance of about 3,000 miles, with a population of more than 200 million and with about 350 different regional cuisines. *Urap,* a spicy, cooling salad suited for the tropical environment, is a popular dish found on several of the islands and is frequently part of feasts for special ceremonial events, such as celebrating a birth.

I've sampled this salad in Bali, and while its flavors are Indonesian—tamarind, coconut, chile—the version that I've included here features the green bean, a vegetable not indigenous to Indonesia, but one that was introduced to the islands by early European explorers some four hundred years ago.

indonesian green bean salad with coconut

(urap)

MAKES 4 SERVINGS

149

¼ cup shredded coconut

¼ pound green beans, trimmed and cut into
    1-inch pieces

½ pound fresh spinach, tough stems removed

2 cups bean sprouts

dressing

1 clove garlic, crushed

1 red chile, sliced

2 thin slices peeled fresh ginger

½ teaspoon sugar

¼ teaspoon salt

1 teaspoon tamarind paste*

1 tablespoon warm water

2 teaspoons fresh lime juice

*For Ingredient Sources, see page 199.

Heat oven to 325 degrees. Spread the shredded coconut on a baking sheet. Toast in 325-degree oven, stirring occasionally, until light golden, about 10 minutes. Set aside.

In a large saucepan of lightly salted boiling water, blanch the green beans until crisp-tender, about 2 minutes. Using a slotted spoon, remove beans to a colander and rinse under cold running water. Drain on paper towels. Add the spinach to the boiling water and blanch until wilted, about 1 minute. Using slotted spoon, remove spinach and place in colander. Add the sprouts to boiling water and blanch 1 minute. Using slotted spoon, remove sprouts and place in a second colander. Rinse under cold running water. Drain on paper towels.

When spinach is cool enough to handle, squeeze out excess liquid. Drain on paper towels. Depending on size of spinach leaves, cut into smaller pieces.

dressing: In a mortar with a pestle, crush together the garlic, chile, ginger, sugar, and salt to make a paste. In a small cup, using your fingertips, mash together the tamarind paste and warm water, removing any seeds, until liquid is brown and thick and pulp is evenly distributed. Stir in garlic-chile paste and the lime juice.

Combine toasted coconut, green beans, spinach, and sprouts in a bowl. Add the dressing and toss well to combine. Serve at room temperature or refrigerate to chill.

150

When you read the list of ingredients for this recipe, you might think you're about to prepare a variation on succotash, which in fact you are. It's a very homey dish that has North American Indian origins. The word "succotash" itself probably derives from the Narragansett Indian word *misickquatash* or *msickquatash*. Look closely at the letters and say the words out loud, and you'll see the connection.

spicy corn and lima beans with tomato

(colache)

MAKES 6 SERVINGS

For a vegetable combination to be considered succotash, it must start with corn and lima beans. From that point on, the addition of seasonings and other vegetables can vary according to regional and cultural influences. The recipe here borrows from the ingredients of the Spanish-American Southwest, which explains the use of chiles.

And then there's the green bean. This seeded pod of the legume family is one of the oldest foods we know, probably going back some four thousand years, which explains why it pops up in recipes from such diverse places as South America, Africa, and Indonesia.

If you have vegetarian friends, this is the dish for them. It's loaded with vegetables that are flavored in a lively fashion with jalapeños, oregano, cumin, and a splash of vinegar.

151

1 tablespoon vegetable oil

1 yellow onion, chopped

2 cloves garlic, finely chopped

1 pound yellow summer squash, trimmed, unpeeled, and cut into 1/2- to 3/4-inch cubes *or* pumpkin, peeled, and cut into same cubes *or* zucchini, trimmed, unpeeled, and cut into same cubes

1/2 pound green beans, trimmed and cut into 1-inch lengths

1 large tomato, seeded and chopped

2 fresh green jalapeño chiles, cored, seeded, and chopped

1 tablespoon dried oregano

1 1/2 teaspoons salt

1 teaspoon ground cumin

1/4 teaspoon black pepper

2 teaspoons cider vinegar

2 tablespoons water

2 cups corn kernels, fresh (about 4 ears) *or* frozen kernels, thawed

1 cup lima beans, fresh *or* frozen, thawed

In a deep, heavy saucepan or Dutch oven, heat the oil. Add the onion and sauté until softened, about 5 minutes. Add the garlic and sauté 1 minute. Add the squash, green beans, tomato, jalapeños, oregano, salt, cumin, pepper, vinegar, and water. Bring to a boil. Cover pot and lower the heat. Simmer until green beans are tender, 10 to 15 minutes.

Add the corn and lima beans. Return to a boil. Then lower heat and simmer, uncovered, until tender, 5 to 10 minutes. Taste and adjust seasoning with oregano, cumin, and/or salt, then serve.

serving tips: This goes well with grilled or roasted meats or egg dishes. To transform into a main dish, stir in—along with the corn and lima beans—8 to 12 ounces cooked pork, shredded cooked chicken, or a strongly flavored ham such as Black Forest. Or stir 8 ounces crumbled farmer's cheese into the hot vegetable mixture at the end, until the cheese is slightly melted.

Throughout South America, there are many local versions of vegetable stew, its contents varying according to what is grown in the area. The dish is called *locro,* and the preparation takes different forms, depending on the country. Sometimes sausage or meat is added. In Ecuador, *locro* is a potato-and-cheese soup (page 156), while in Argentina it is this thicker stew made with squash.

argentine squash stew with corn and cheese

(locro)

MAKES 6 SERVINGS

This recipe is based on one from the family cook of an Argentine friend, whose business took him back and forth between Buenos Aires and New York City. Even though *locro* is usually served as a main course, with rice on the side, my friend was very fond of beef (as many Argentines are), and he often preferred *locro* as a side dish to his grilled meat.

153

2 tablespoons vegetable oil

1 medium-size yellow onion, chopped

1 teaspoon ground cumin

4 cloves garlic, chopped

1 to 2 fresh jalapeño chiles, cored, seeded, and finely chopped

2 pounds acorn squash *or* butternut squash, peeled, seeded, and cut into 1-inch cubes (4 to 5 cups)

1 can (5 ounces) evaporated milk

¾ teaspoon salt

1 cup corn kernels, fresh (1 ear) *or* frozen, thawed

¾ cup crumbled *queso fresco* (firmly packed fresh cheese) *or* fresh feta cheese *or* farmer's cheese

½ cup peas, fresh *or* frozen, thawed

½ teaspoon white pepper

In a large skillet, heat the oil. Add the onion and cumin and sauté until softened, 6 to 8 minutes. Add the garlic and jalapeños and sauté 1 minute. Add the squash, evaporated milk, and salt. Cover skillet and cook until the squash is almost tender, about 25 minutes.

Stir in the corn and cheese and cook, covered, 5 minutes. Stir in the peas and cook, covered, 5 minutes. Season with the white pepper, and serve.

make-ahead tip: This stew can be made ahead and refrigerated for a day or two, and then gently reheated in a saucepan over medium-low heat. Avoid stirring too much, so the squash doesn't get mashed.

155

Harrison, New Jersey, is a town on the Passaic River across from Newark. A walk down its main street takes you past an assortment of restaurants: Brazilian, Portuguese, Ecuadorian, Italian, and Polish. One

ecuadorian potato-cheese soup with avocado

MAKES 8 SERVINGS

of the Ecuadorian restaurants serves breakfast, lunch, and dinner, seven days a week, and on Sundays, it is full of young families surrounded by huge platters of food. It was there that I discovered this richly satisfying soup with its bright, sunny color. It's called *locro,* but it's different from the Argentine *locro* (page 153), and also contains most of the same ingredients as *Papas a la Huancaina* (page 144) from Peru, Ecuador's neighbor to the south. When a Danish friend of mine tasted this soup, she remarked that it reminded her of a similar soup that she grew up with in Denmark, but hers had peas.

For a meatier version, I've made this soup with a pound of shredded cooked chicken stirred in.

2 tablespoons unsalted butter

1 medium-size yellow onion, chopped

1 teaspoon Hungarian sweet paprika

1/4 teaspoon turmeric

4 cups cold water

2 teaspoons salt

1/4 teaspoon black pepper

4 large Yukon Gold potatoes (about 2 pounds) *or* other boiling potatoes, peeled and cut into 1/2-inch-thick slices

2 cups light cream

2 cups corn kernels, fresh *or* frozen, thawed

1 cup crumbled *queso blanco* (firmly packed fresh cheese) *or* crumbled farmer's cheese *or* grated Muenster cheese (about 1/4 pound)

2 medium-size ripe avocados

Snipped fresh chives *or* fresh cilantro leaves, for garnish

In a large saucepan, heat the butter over medium heat. Add the onion, paprika, and turmeric and sauté until onion is softened, about 4 to 5 minutes. Add the water, salt, and pepper. Bring to a boil. Add the potatoes. Lower heat and simmer, covered, until potatoes are tender, about 25 minutes.

Break up potatoes into smaller pieces with a fork or wooden spoon. Stir in the cream and corn and cook until heated through and corn is tender, about 4 minutes. Stir in the cheese and heat until melted, about 1 minute.

Halve, peel, and pit the avocados. Slice crosswise. Place avocado pieces in soup bowls. Ladle soup over the avocado slices, garnish with snipped fresh chives or cilantro leaves, and serve.

I once lived with a friend on twelve acres of very tillable pasture land, and had visions of growing boutique lettuces and vegetables and raising sheep and goats. The closest I got to this dream of an agrarian life was a smallish vegetable garden that did actually produce quite a bit, once I surrounded it with a high wall of chicken wire to keep out the deer. I grew several different kinds of tomatoes. One year I even sprouted heirloom seeds indoors in late March and put the young plants in the ground in early May. That year, I harvested quite a crop of tomatoes, of different flavors, sizes, and colors. I also grew lots of sweet red peppers, so it wasn't long before I began making an early version of this recipe, the peppers' sweetness coupling naturally with the acid-sweetness of the tomatoes. And I've always loved the flavor of fennel's crunchy fresh bulbs and aromatic seeds—they have an earthiness that appeals to me—so I've incorporated the seeds here.

tomato-and-
sweet-red-pepper soup

MAKES 4 SERVINGS

Did you know that the tomato is originally from South America, and that it spread up through Central America to Mexico, where the Aztecs incorporated it into their cooking? Then in the 1500s it was transported across the Atlantic by the Spanish, just as the Portuguese were opening up the spice routes to Indonesia and India. Early fusion cooking?

You can easily double or triple this recipe and freeze the soup in batches to have it at the ready.

159

2 tablespoons butter

1 tablespoon olive oil

1 large yellow onion, halved and sliced crosswise

4 tomatoes (about 2 pounds), cored, peeled, seeded, and chopped (about 3 cups) *or* 1 can (28 ounces) peeled whole tomatoes, seeded and chopped

2 sweet red peppers, cored, seeded, and chopped

3/4 teaspoon fennel seeds, crushed

1/2 teaspoon salt

1/4 teaspoon black pepper

2 cans (14.5 ounces each) chicken broth

In a large saucepan, heat the butter and oil over medium heat. Add the onion and sauté until softened, about 8 minutes. Stir in the tomatoes and red peppers and cook over medium-low heat, stirring occasionally, until the juices have evaporated, 30 to 45 minutes.

Stir the crushed fennel seeds, salt, pepper, and chicken broth into tomato mixture. Bring to a boil. Then lower heat and simmer 25 minutes, stirring occasionally.

Strain soup through a sieve over a large bowl. Working in batches, puree the solids in a food processor. Return strained liquid to saucepan. Whisk in puree. Gently reheat. Ladle the soup into soup bowls, and serve.

make-ahead tip: This soup can be refrigerated for up to 3 days, or frozen for up to 1 month.

One of my favorite breads comes from Zito's bakery in New York City's Greenwich Village. It's a simple Italian loaf with a very crunchy crust and a coarse-textured interior. When I lived in the neighborhood, I was always there early on Saturday morning to pick up a few loaves still warm from the oven. A friend of mine, a real carbohydrate junkie, would often devour half a loaf of Zito's by the time he had walked a couple of blocks on his way home.

zucchini *garbure* with *rouille*

MAKES 8 SERVINGS

This liking for bread seems to be universal, and one that has been with us since the New Stone Age, when humans domesticated plants and animals. In many cuisines, bread is used as a thickener in soups and other brothy dishes, and is also a way to extend and add bulk to a small amount of ingredients. This vegetable stew is based on Italian *ribollite* and French *garbures* that I've eaten over the years, which are either vegetable- or meat-based stews thickened with bread. For this *garbure,* each serving is garnished with a dollop of a fiery *rouille,* a Provençale mayonnaise flavored with roasted red peppers, garlic, and crushed red-pepper flakes.

In order to reduce your work time in the kitchen, prepare the zucchini and tomatoes while the onions are slowly sautéing. To keep the dish vegetarian, use water or vegetable broth rather than chicken broth.

161

vegetables

6 slices stale Italian bread or other
  coarse-textured bread, ½ inch thick, from a
  large round loaf (or fresh bread will do)
2 tablespoons olive oil
1 pound yellow onions, sliced
1 can (28 ounces) peeled whole tomatoes
½ teaspoon dried thyme
½ teaspoon dried basil
¼ teaspoon salt
¼ teaspoon black pepper
3 cloves garlic, chopped
1 pound zucchini, trimmed, halved lengthwise,
  and cut crosswise into half-moon–shaped
  slices
2 cups shredded mozzarella cheese (½ pound)
1 can (14.5 ounces) chicken broth

rouille

3 cloves garlic, finely chopped
½ teaspoon salt
3 large pieces bottled roasted red peppers,
  drained
¼ teaspoon crushed red-pepper flakes
½ cup mayonnaise

Preheat oven to 300 degrees. Bake the bread slices on a baking sheet until crisp but not browned, about 5 minutes per side. Remove bread from oven and increase temperature to 375 degrees.

In a large nonstick skillet, heat the oil. Add the onion and sauté over low heat until softened and golden, 20 minutes; don't let brown.

Drain the tomatoes over a bowl, reserving liquid. Chop tomatoes into small pieces. In a small cup, mix the thyme, basil, salt, and pepper.

Spread ½ cup of the onions over bottom of 6-quart oven-proof casserole. Top with 2 slices of the toasted bread, half the remaining onions, half the tomatoes, half the spice mixture, half the garlic, half the zucchini, and half the cheese. Repeat layering, ending with 2 slices of bread. Pour the chicken broth and ½ cup reserved tomato juice over contents of pot. Cover pot. Bring to a boil on stovetop.

Place casserole in 300-degree oven. Bake 30 minutes or until zucchini is tender. Uncover pot. Bake until bread on top is crisped, 15 minutes.

rouille: Using the side of a chef's knife, smash together the garlic and salt on a cutting board to make a paste. Scrape into a small bowl. In a food processor, puree the red peppers. Stir into garlic mixture, along with the red-pepper flakes and mayonnaise.

Spoon *garbure* into soup bowls. Top with a dab of *rouille,* and serve.

serving tip: Add a green salad, tossed with a balsamic vinaigrette.

make-ahead tip: This casserole can be assembled earlier and refrigerated. Add some extra baking time if it's going straight from the refrigerator to the oven.

163

During the summer of 1969, I was traveling by motorcycle down the Dalmatian coastline of Yugoslavia on my way to meet friends in Athens—I was part of that generation who explored the world in the late '60s. Yugoslavia was a quiet country still controlled by Marshal Tito. As I stopped at a passport check on the highway near Dubrovnik—there were several such checks along the road—I experienced one of those memorable moments that life often springs on us. When the guard saw my American passport, he grinned and pointed to the sky. I was puzzled, and then I realized what he meant. Neil Armstrong had just walked on the moon.

albanian cornmeal pie with scallions and feta cheese

MAKES 6 SERVINGS

To get to Greece, I had to detour around Albania, which was off-limits to Americans. The road, what there was of it, was mainly gravel, making a speed of more than five or ten kilometers per hour risky business, since anything faster would result in a spinout, as it in fact did when I tried to push my luck. I was famished and exhausted. Somewhere in the mountains of the Kosovo region, I stopped at a roadside food hut—who knows why it was there, except that this was the *only* road that skirted Albania. This was my lunch break, and what I ate was a coarse cornbread, flavored and moistened with a fresh cheese. I'll never forget the simple, satisfying flavors of that meal. It was a life-saver.

I learned later that two of the mainstays of Albanian-influenced cooking—shaped by the Turks, Greeks, and Italians—are corn and cheese (cheese usually made from goat's and sheep's milk). This, then, is my adaptation of that simple meal that provided a much-needed, if brief, moment of pleasure. As an alternative, I've also made the pie with farmer's cheese for the topping, rather than the feta, and half a cup of oil-cured olives, such as Kalamata, pitted and halved.

164

Unsalted butter, for greasing pan

1½ cups yellow cornmeal

12 ounces small-curd cottage cheese

4 eggs, lightly beaten

1 bunch scallions (about 9), chopped
    (about 1 cup)

¼ cup (½ stick) unsalted butter, melted

¾ teaspoon dried thyme

¼ teaspoon salt

4 ounces feta cheese

Heat oven to 400 degrees. Butter a 9-inch pie plate.

In a medium bowl, stir together the cornmeal, cottage cheese, eggs, scallions, melted butter, thyme, and salt. Scrape into prepared pie plate and spread evenly. Sprinkle the feta over the top.

Bake in 400-degree oven until golden brown, set, and slightly puffed, about 45 minutes. Let stand 15 minutes, then serve warm.

serving tips: This makes a satisfying main course with a green salad or juicy ripe tomatoes, sliced and seasoned with coarsely ground black pepper and a drizzle of olive oil. Or cut into wedges and serve as you would cornbread, with soups, stews, roasts, egg dishes, or wherever an assertively flavored bread would work. Use leftovers together with smoked ham or thinly sliced sausage to make small sandwiches.

Americans who grew up in the 1950s and '60s with this classic dish developed a special yen for it, and their nostalgic "romance" with both the made-from-scratch casserole and the pre-packaged variety has continued. The appeal of noodles and cheese with its comforting gooey-ness accounts for the dish's popularity. Similar pairings occur in Mexican cooking with tortillas and cheese, and in South America with potatoes and cheese.

mac 'n' cheese with chipotle

MAKES 8 SERVINGS

I can chart my own culinary development by looking at how my taste for mac 'n'cheese has changed over the years. In the beginning I went crazy for an almost puddinglike cheese casserole that just happened to have a few noodles in it, and I used only cheddar. As time went on, I began to prefer slightly drier versions, with a little Monterey Jack stirred in for added smoothness. Then I hit my Maytag blue/Stilton/Gorgonzola phase. These were strongly flavored macs. This indulgence didn't last long—it was too much of a good thing, even for me. Next, I began to experiment with various combinations of cheeses, always adding a little Parmesan for an edge. And then I discovered the chipotle in *adobo* (see *Adobo,* page xiii), and here is the result.

You can find the chipotle packed in a can with the *adobo* sauce in Latin American markets or in the Spanish section of your supermarket. Also, you can substitute *queso blanco* or *queso quesadilla*—mild Spanish cheeses—for the Monterey Jack.

Vegetable oil, for greasing baking dish

2 teaspoons salt

1 pound cavatappi pasta *or* elbow twist pasta

⅓ cup all-purpose flour

4 cups whole milk

1 tablespoon Dijon mustard

1 canned chipotle chile in *adobo* sauce,
   seeded and chopped

1 cup shredded sharp cheddar cheese (4 ounces)

½ cup shredded Monterey Jack cheese
   (2 ounces)

¼ cup grated Parmesan cheese

1 can (14.5 ounces) peeled whole tomatoes,
   drained and chopped

½ cup chopped scallions (about 4 scallions)

½ cup fresh bread crumbs (1 slice)

Heat oven to 375 degrees. Lightly grease a 13 × 9 × 2-inch baking dish or other 3-quart casserole with vegetable oil. Bring a large pot of water to a boil and add 1 teaspoon of the salt. Add the pasta and cook until firm but tender, about 8 minutes.

Meanwhile, in a medium-size saucepan, place the flour. Gradually stir in the milk until well blended. Bring to a boil, stirring occasionally. Lower heat and simmer, stirring frequently, until thickened, about 2 minutes. Stir in the mustard, chipotle, cheddar, Monterey Jack, and 2 tablespoons of the Parmesan and cook until cheese is melted.

Drain pasta. Return to cooking pot and add the cheese sauce, tomatoes, scallions, and remaining 1 teaspoon salt. Scrape into prepared baking dish. In a small bowl, stir together the bread crumbs and remaining 2 tablespoons Parmesan, and sprinkle evenly over pasta mixture.

Bake in 375-degree oven for 20 minutes or until bubbly and topping is browned. Let stand 10 minutes, then serve.

serving tip: For a crisp side salad, dress blanched green beans with a lime-juice vinaigrette.

make-ahead tip: Assemble the mac 'n' cheese without the bread-crumb topping and refrigerate, covered. To serve, sprinkle with topping and bake as above, increasing the baking time if the casserole is going directly from the refrigerator to the oven. Leftovers can be reheated, covered, in a 350-degree oven or in a microwave oven.

Olive oil and eggplant appear with great frequency in Turkish cooking, a cuisine shaped by the chefs of the royal kitchens in the Topkapi Palace during four hundred years of the Ottoman Empire. It is not unusual

turkish eggplant stuffed with tomato, garlic, and parsley

MAKES 4 SERVINGS

for the cooking of a royal court to evolve as a codified cuisine, as chefs continually attempt to titillate the appetites of their rulers and at the same time satisfy the hunger of the thousands of people who make up the court. This phenomenon occurred at the courts of the emperors of Rome, Louis XIV in France, and the emperors of the imperial city of Hue in Vietnam.

The following recipe is based on a well-known Turkish eggplant dish called *imam bayildi,* which translates as "the prayer man fainted," and is from a category of meatless preparations that rely on good-quality olive oil. Several explanations are offered for the origin of the dish, but two stories seem to be the most popular. In the first, a Muslim prayer leader was so overwhelmed by the deliciousness of the eggplant that he swooned with pleasure after savoring a bite of it. The second tale describes the *imam* collapsing when he realizes the expense of the extravagant amount of olive oil used.

Perhaps not leaving well enough alone, I've tinkered with the classic recipe by adding a little chopped fresh dill and grated citrus zest.

169

vegetables

4 baby eggplants *or* Japanese eggplants
(about 1¼ pounds total)
Coarse salt
¼ cup olive oil
1 small yellow onion, finely chopped
8 cloves garlic, finely chopped
1 small tomato, cored and chopped
(about ¾ cup)
½ cup chopped fresh parsley, plus extra
for garnish
2 tablespoons chopped fresh dill
½ teaspoon sugar
½ teaspoon salt
2 teaspoons grated lemon zest and a squeeze
of juice *or* 2 teaspoons grated orange zest
and a squeeze of juice
¼ cup hot water, plus more as needed

Using a small paring knife, peel parallel "stripes" lengthwise on each eggplant, alternating purple skin with exposed white. Cut a lengthwise slit halfway to three-quarters of the way through each eggplant, to within a ½ inch of each end. Salt each eggplant and let stand on paper towels 45 minutes to release bitterness and some excess moisture. Rinse eggplants well under cold running water. Thoroughly pat dry with paper towels.

Meanwhile, prepare stuffing. In a large skillet, heat 1 tablespoon of the oil. Add the onion and sauté until softened, 5 to 10 minutes. Add the garlic and sauté until fragrant, about 1 minute. Scrape into a bowl. Add the tomato, parsley, dill, sugar, salt, and citrus zest and juice to the onion-garlic mixture.

When eggplants have been rinsed and dried, heat 2 tablespoons of the oil in same skillet. Add eggplants and sauté until golden brown on all sides, about 15 minutes total. Remove to a plate.

Heat oven to 375 degrees. Arrange eggplants, slit side up, in a small baking dish. Spread open eggplants. Fill each with stuffing. Drizzle with remaining oil. Add ¼ cup hot water to baking dish. Cover baking dish tightly with aluminum foil.

Bake in 375-degree oven until eggplants are tender, about 1 hour. Check from time to time, making sure there is still a little liquid in the bottom of the baking dish. Add more water as needed. Remove from oven and let cool. Serve at room temperature or chilled, sprinkled with a little more chopped fresh parsley for garnish.

serving tips: These eggplants are good on their own as a light lunch with crusty bread, an assortment of cured olives, and a green salad, or as a make-ahead accompaniment to grilled or roasted meats.

As I mentioned in the Introduction to this book, I discovered the flavor of fish grilled over fennel branches long ago on the island of Corfu. After that, it was just a short leap to learning how to incorporate fennel seeds and fresh fennel into my own cooking.

cream of fennel soup

MAKES 6 SERVINGS

This recipe is based on a soup I was served at La Pyramide, Fernand Point's legendary three-star restaurant in Vienne, France. There was nothing fancy about that version, and it was as simple as any *bonne femme* home-cooked rendition. By the time I had a chance to go to La Pyramide, Monsieur had died, and Madame was then in charge, still maintaining the high standards her husband had championed.

My version has few ingredients and only one spice in addition to the basic salt and pepper. The predominant flavor is that of the fennel, with no intricate parade of tastes as you take a spoonful, as there is in some of my recipes from Southeast Asia. Everything in the recipe is there just to accent the fennel. The soup is quite soothing and subtle.

The fennel available in today's markets is sweet fennel; its origins have been traced to Italy and the south of France. But through the Arab trade routes, both the stalk and especially the seed gained popularity in the Middle East, and then eventually spread to China via India, in much the same way spices traveled from India and Indonesia to Europe.

When at the suggestion of a friend I tried this cold, I discovered that it also makes a delicious summer soup.

172

3 large fennel bulbs (about 3 pounds)

2 tablespoons olive oil

1 yellow onion, thinly sliced

1 can (14.5 ounces) chicken broth, plus
    cold water to equal 4 cups, plus more
    water as needed

1½ teaspoons salt

¼ teaspoon white pepper

¾ cup heavy cream

⅛ teaspoon ground nutmeg

Fresh dill (optional)

Trim the stalks from the fennel bulbs and save for future use, such as in salads or for braising. Reserve some of the feathery fronds for a garnish, if desired. Halve the bulbs through the root end, cut out the core, and thinly slice halves crosswise.

In a large saucepan, heat the olive oil. Add the onion and sauté until it just begins to brown, about 5 minutes. Add sliced fennel, plus about 2 tablespoons of the broth with water. Cover pan and "sweat" or cook the fennel over medium heat until it is slightly tender, 10 to 15 minutes, stirring from time to time. Add the salt and white pepper. Add the remaining chicken broth with water to cover the fennel, adding more water if needed. Bring to a boil. Lower heat, partially cover saucepan, and simmer until fennel is very tender, about 30 minutes.

Drain fennel in a colander set over a large bowl and reserve the cooking liquid. Working in batches, spoon solids into a food processor. Process, adding as much of the cooking liquid as needed to make a smooth puree. Wipe out saucepan with a paper towel and transfer puree to pan. Stir in enough of reserved cooking liquid for desired consistency. (My preference is to keep the soup slightly thick.) Stir in the heavy cream and nutmeg. Gently reheat, and serve garnished with fennel fronds and chopped fresh dill, if desired. Or refrigerate soup and serve chilled.

serving tip: This soup is delicious either warm or chilled, depending on the weather and your taste. It makes a perfect light lunch or a first course, with a small salad of bitter greens, such as radicchio, Belgian endive, and/or kale.

173

vegetables

Ask a crowd of people what their favorite one-pot dish is to cook, and at least two or three will holler out, "Chili!" Just witness all the chili cook-offs that take place every year. And there are so many different types of chili: very spicy, not so spicy, with tomato, without meat, with vegetables and meat, with one bean, with several beans, with chocolate (as in a *mole*), and on and on.

two-bean vegetarian chili with zucchini

MAKES 12 SERVINGS

What I've developed here is a vegetarian chili that many people will assume is full of meat if you don't tell them otherwise. There are two secrets. The first is that the lentils become so soft during the long simmering that they thicken the chili, imparting a satisfying, meaty texture. And the second trick is the use of a mushroom soy sauce, a dark soy, which adds subtle depth of flavor, much the same way a double bass adds a deep richness to an orchestral piece. Music and food—no great stretch when you're talking about pleasure.

This is a dish that gets better as the days go on.

1 cup (about 7 ounces) dried pinto beans,
   picked over and rinsed

1 cup (about 7 ounces) dried red kidney beans,
   picked over and rinsed

16 cups cold water

2 tablespoons vegetable oil

2 large yellow onions, finely chopped

6 cloves garlic, finely chopped

2 carrots, peeled and diced

1 rib celery, diced

2 cups (13 ounces) dried lentils, picked over
   and rinsed

3 tablespoons chili powder (hotness depending
   on your taste)

2 tablespoons Hungarian sweet paprika

2 tablespoons dried oregano

4 teaspoons ground coriander

1 can (28 ounces) peeled whole tomatoes
   with their liquid, chopped

2 sweet red peppers, cored, seeded, and chopped

1/2 pound zucchini, trimmed and cut into
   1/4-inch cubes

1/3 cup mushroom soy sauce* or regular dark
   soy sauce

1/2 teaspoon salt

*For Ingredient Sources, see page 199.

In a large bowl, combine the pinto and kidney beans and 10 cups of the cold water. Let stand overnight in a cool place. Drain in a colander, rinse, and drain again.

In a large saucepan or pot, heat the oil. Add the onions, garlic, carrots, and celery and sauté until softened, 8 to 10 minutes. Add the drained beans, lentils, chili powder, paprika, oregano, coriander, tomatoes, and the remaining 6 cups water. Bring to a boil. Lower heat and simmer, uncovered, stirring occasionally, 1 1/2 hours.

Add the sweet red peppers, zucchini, and soy sauce. Simmer, uncovered, until beans are very tender and lentils are falling apart, about another 2 hours. If the chili becomes too dry, add a little more water and/or partially cover the pot. Stir in the salt at the end, and serve.

serving tips: If you like your vegetables a little more resistant to the bite, add the sweet red pepper and zucchini for just the last 45 minutes of cooking time. Top each bowl of chili with sour cream, salsa, and grated cheese such as an aged manchego or Parmesan, or whatever seems to make sense for your own taste.

vegetables

desserts

My mother made homemade cheesecake for special occasions, and it was always a cause for great excitement, at least on my part. When the time came, she pulled out a tattered recipe card from her file box, and the kitchen counter became piled high with blocks of cream cheese. I also remember that when the cake was in the oven we had to walk very quietly in the house—no heavy-footing and no slamming the back door as we went out to play. Her strategy must have worked, because her cakes never had any cracks in the top. She always made the same version, and it was a very rich, very dense New York–style cheesecake, with a firm texture.

pumpkin cheesecake with persimmon glaze

MAKES 12 SERVINGS

I often get writing assignments from food magazines specializing in low-calorie and/or low-fat food. So, given my fondness for rich dishes, it's always a challenge for me to reshuffle my personal food tastes. This recipe is based on one that was part of a low-fat Thanksgiving menu I developed several years ago. What follows here, though, is the full-fat version, in the tradition of that cheesecake my mother made years ago. However, as with most things I do, I couldn't resist fiddling. This is a pumpkin variation with a little sour cream stirred in, and a level of spicing that is not overpowering. And the topping is very easy: pureed persimmon that sets up easily as a shiny glaze without any thickener. The sweet-tartness of the persimmon goes perfectly with the pumpkin-and-cheese combination in the cake.

I don't use a water bath for this cheesecake. What I do to prevent any major cracking is to carefully run a thin knife or metal icing spatula around the side of the cake to loosen it as soon as it comes out of the oven, so when the cake contracts as it cools, it doesn't stick to the side of the pan.

179

desserts

crust

2 teaspoons unsalted butter, at room
temperature, for greasing pan

16 gingersnap cookies

2 tablespoons unsalted butter, melted

filling

3 packages (8 ounces each) cream cheese,
at room temperature

1/2 cup sour cream

1 cup sugar

5 eggs

1 can (15 ounces) solid-pack pumpkin puree
(not pie filling)

2 teaspoons pure vanilla extract

1/2 teaspoon ground cinnamon

1/4 teaspoon ground cloves

1/4 teaspoon ground ginger

1/4 teaspoon salt

glaze

1 persimmon (Hachiya or Fuyu)

crust: Heat oven to 325 degrees. Butter a 9-inch springform pan. In a food processor, finely grind the gingersnaps. Add the melted butter and process until combined. Scrape mixture out of workbowl and pat evenly over bottom of pan.

Bake crust in 325-degree oven until dark in color, 10 to 15 minutes. Remove to a wire rack and let cool completely.

filling: Heat oven again to 325 degrees. In a large bowl, beat together the cream cheese and sour cream until smooth. Beat in the sugar until smooth. Beat in the eggs, one at a time, beating well after each. Beat in the pumpkin, vanilla, cinnamon, cloves, ginger, and salt. Pour into prepared crust.

Bake in 325-degree oven for 1 1/4 hours or until just set in center. If browning too quickly, tent loosely with aluminum foil. After you take the cheesecake out of the oven, gently run a thin knife around the outside edge of the cake. Let cake cool in pan on wire rack. Refrigerate, covered, overnight.

glaze: Peel the persimmon and core. Cut into chunks. Place in a food processor and puree. Release side of springform pan and remove. Spread glaze over top of cheesecake. Refrigerate until glaze is firm, about 1 hour, then serve.

180

I grew up loving mashed bananas in a bowl, puddings of every kind, and whipped cream on anything, especially the beaters. Beater-licking for me was a ritual—I ran my tongue over one beater sprocket at a time, taking my time and enjoying the sweet richness.

double chocolate pudding

MAKES 4 SERVINGS

When I collaborated with Richard Sax in 1980 on a cookbook, *Cooking Great Meals Every Day,* we decided we needed a chocolate pudding recipe for it. Because of my love of puddings, I volunteered to develop this recipe. So, I began to work on it, and work on it, and work on it, but I just couldn't get it quite right. The manuscript was due on a Monday, and I was still melting chocolate the Friday before. I don't remember if at that point I was fiddling with the amount of milk or the cornstarch.

But I do remember the afternoon itself. It was drizzling outside, and I was living in a small, one-bedroom fifth-floor walkup in New York City's Greenwich Village. The kitchen was workable, although the stove was tiny. But there was a huge window facing south that flooded the room with light, even on a drizzly day. The typewriter—there were not a lot of PCs or Macs back then—was sitting on the desk in the next room, waiting. Well, whatever the final adjustment was, it worked. The texture and taste were what I wanted—creamy richness with a deep chocolate flavor. That pudding just oozed off the spoon. I went to the typewriter, made the corrections, and inserted the page into the manuscript. And here is that recipe.

desserts

double chocolate pudding

2 1/4 cups milk
1/2 cup sugar
Pinch salt
2 tablespoons cornstarch, sifted
2 tablespoons unsweetened cocoa powder
1 egg
2 egg yolks
5 ounces semisweet chocolate, cut into pieces
2 tablespoons unsalted butter, cut into pieces
1 teaspoon pure vanilla extract
Lightly whipped cream

In a heavy saucepan, combine 2 cups of the milk, 1/4 cup of the sugar, and the salt. Place over medium heat, and bring just to a boil. Remove from heat.

In a small bowl, stir together the cornstarch, cocoa powder, and remaining 1/4 cup sugar. Whisk remaining 1/4 cup milk into cornstarch mixture until well blended and smooth. Slowly whisk in hot milk mixture. Return to saucepan. Gently boil, stirring constantly and scraping bottom of pan, until very thick, about 2 minutes.

In a small bowl, whisk together the egg and yolks. Slowly whisk in 1 cup of the hot cocoa mixture. Whisk back into cocoa mixture in pan. Cook, whisking constantly, over medium heat, until mixture becomes slightly thicker, about 2 minutes; do not let boil. Scrape into a clean bowl. Place a piece of waxed paper directly on the surface to prevent skin from forming. Let cool slightly on a wire rack.

Melt the chocolate in top of a double boiler over simmering water, or in a small saucepan over very low heat, or in a microwave-safe bowl in a microwave oven. Stir in the butter until blended. Let cool slightly—the chocolate should remain pourable. Whisk melted chocolate into thickened egg mixture. Stir in the vanilla. Cool in bowl on a wire rack. Cover bowl and refrigerate until chilled, about 2 hours. Serve with whipped cream.

make-ahead tip: The pudding can be refrigerated, covered, for a day or two.

182

I didn't really discover fresh figs until relatively late in life. There is a market called Balducci's not far from where I live in New York City. Run by the Balducci family for many years, it was a truly amazing emporium full of smoked fishes and sausages, dried pasta, produce, fresh fish, aged meats, poultry, and on and on. But it was sold recently, and now the bags of upscale snack chips are creeping into the aisles.

roasted figs with candied ginger and crème fraîche

MAKES 4 SERVINGS

One night about twenty years ago, I was standing in the crowded checkout line, which wound through part of the produce section. I looked over, and there were baskets of the most perfect-looking fresh figs. I was hooked. I picked up a basket, ran over to the deli counter to get a quarter pound of very thinly sliced imported prosciutto, and grabbed a lemon—and that was my dinner.

The fig, like the potato, is one of those foods that have crossed oceans. Its origins can be traced back to Asia Minor and Mediterranean countries; the first cultivation probably occurred in Egypt around 3000 B.C. Then, toward the latter half of the eighteenth century, Spanish Franciscan missionaries introduced the fig to North America when they established an outpost in San Diego—hence the name Mission figs. There are several varieties of figs, available in the markets from early summer to late fall—and they all work well in this recipe.

The ingredients in this dessert create a perfect play of flavor against flavor: the sweet-tartness of the fresh fig, the sugary heat of the candied ginger, and the seductive creaminess of the crème fraîche.

183

desserts

2 teaspoons unsalted butter, at room
    temperature, for greasing dish
8 ripe figs, halved lengthwise
1 tablespoon sugar
1 tablespoon chopped candied ginger
1 teaspoon fresh lemon juice
¼ cup crème fraîche *or* mascarpone
Grated lemon zest, for garnish

Heat oven to 400 degrees. Use the butter to grease a small baking dish, pie plate, or roasting pan just large enough to hold the figs. Place figs in dish and turn them around in the butter to coat. Then arrange them, cut side up. Sprinkle figs with the sugar, then the ginger.

Bake in 400-degree oven until figs are hot and cooked through, 10 to 12 minutes. Remove pan to a wire rack. Sprinkle figs with the lemon juice and let stand 5 minutes. Serve with the crème fraîche or mascarpone, and garnish with the lemon zest.

I first sampled black rice pudding on the island of Bali in Indonesia. In fact, I tasted two versions, almost back to back. The first one was served at a special banquet one evening at the Bongkasa Village. We were there to eat, and also to watch a riveting outdoor performance of the Kecak Dance, inspired by the *Kecak Ganda Sari,* a mythical tale based on the Hindu epic *Ramayana.* In this spectacular excerpt, a chorus of about seventy-five young, bare-chested men formed concentric circles as they wildly chanted syncopated bursts of a rapid clicking sound mimicking monkeys—"chak-chak-chak-chak"—while moving their upper bodies rhythmically in contrasting movement. Mesmerizing indeed.

asian
black rice pudding

MAKES 6 SERVINGS

The very next morning I had black rice pudding for breakfast at Naughty Nuri's Warung, a roadside restaurant in Ubud, a town in south-central Bali that has a large number of shops and galleries showcasing Balinese wood carving, painting, and other arts and crafts. While it was a spot for Balinese cooking in a homey setting, it also specialized in feasts of grilled ribs and sausages out in the backyard, which seemed to draw a lot of the American expats in the area. The owners are a married couple: Nuri is Indonesian and her husband, Brian, is from New York.

My version of black rice pudding is made with Thai black sticky rice, also called glutinous rice. The outer coating of the rice grain is hard and black-colored, while the center is white. Black rice takes considerably more time to cook than white rice, and turns a deep purple color. The palm sugar adds a buttery sweetness, almost like maple sugar, and the creamy coconut milk sauce makes a smooth, rich contrast to the slightly "toothy" rice.

coconut sauce

1 can (14 ounces) coconut milk

Pinch salt

pudding

1 cup Thai black sticky rice*

Cold water, for soaking

4 cups cold water

5 to 7 tablespoons palm sugar* *or* packed
    light-brown sugar

*For Ingredient Sources, see page 199.

coconut sauce: In a medium-size saucepan, combine the coconut milk and salt. Simmer, stirring, until the liquid has thickened slightly, 15 to 20 minutes. Pour into a small bowl and let cool. Then cover and refrigerate.

pudding: Rinse the rice in a sieve under cold running water. Place in a bowl and add enough cold water to cover the rice by at least 1 inch. Let stand in a cool place for 8 hours or overnight. Drain rice.

In a heavy saucepan, combine the rice and the 4 cups water. Cover pan and bring to a boil. Lower heat, and maintain a gentle simmer until all the liquid is absorbed and rice is tender but still toothy, $1\frac{1}{2}$ to $1\frac{3}{4}$ hours. The texture of the pudding should be very thick, but still spoonable. Toward the end of cooking, be sure to stir occasionally to prevent any scorching or sticking on bottom of pot. If rice looks as though it's becoming too dry, add a little more water. Remove pot from heat and stir in palm sugar. Let cool.

To serve, spoon rice pudding into individual bowls. Spoon a little coconut milk sauce over each serving and let each diner stir it into the rice.

serving tips: Breakfast, dessert, or snack time—this pudding is deliciously appropriate for all three occasions. The pudding itself can be served chilled, at room temperature, or slightly warmed. I prefer the coconut milk sauce slightly chilled, but it is also very good at room temperature.

desserts

I grew up with custards, tapioca, and puddings. So when I travel, I'm always looking for new ways to make them. In Southeast Asia, especially in Indonesia, Malaysia, and Thailand, there are endless versions of coconut custard sweetened with palm sugar. I've tasted many of these, and the flavor often reminds me of our American coconut custard pie. They are usually made with coconut milk, one of my favorite ingredients. I like it for its richness, smoothness, and vaguely vanilla taste, and for the fact that it serves as a wonderful background to a lot of other more assertive flavors. That's why coconut milk is often found in the complicated curries and other spicy dishes of Southeast Asia. In South America, evaporated milk is frequently used for the same purpose.

bread pudding with pineapple and coconut milk

MAKES 8 SERVINGS

There is currently a trend in New York City restaurants to take old-fashioned bread pudding and make it with coconut milk—and with pineapple. A few years back, just a block from Washington Square in New York City, there was a restaurant called the Coach House, owned by Leon Lianides. He was always there in the dining room, keeping an eye on his dinner guests. His bread pudding was a favorite, more custardy than bready.

To replicate the flavor of the coconut custards I've sampled in Southeast Asia and to capture it in a bread pudding, I've started with the recipe for the Coach House bread pudding. Fiddling with the proportions, I've added coconut milk, chunks of pineapple, and a little sprinkling of candied ginger.

The trick with this bread pudding, as with any custard, is to make sure not to overbake it. Remove the pudding from the oven at the time specified in the recipe. The center may still seem a little too wiggly, but that's the way it should be; it will firm up as it cools.

Butter for greasing baking dish
5 eggs
4 egg yolks
1 cup sugar
$\frac{1}{8}$ teaspoon salt
4 cups milk
1 cup coconut milk
1 teaspoon pure vanilla extract
1 cup $\frac{1}{2}$-inch cubes fresh pineapple *or* 1 can
    (8 ounces) pineapple chunks, in juice, drained
    and patted dry with paper towels
2 teaspoons chopped candied ginger (optional)
12 slices ($\frac{1}{4}$ inch thick) day-old French bread,
    crusts trimmed

Heat oven to 375 degrees. Butter an $8 \times 8 \times 2$-inch baking dish or other 2-quart baking dish. In a large bowl, beat together the eggs, egg yolks, sugar, and salt until well blended.

In a small, heavy saucepan, heat the milk and coconut milk over medium heat until small bubbles appear around edges of pan. Gradually stir scalded milk mixture into yolk mixture. Stir in the vanilla.

Spoon the pineapple chunks into bottom of prepared baking dish. Sprinkle the chopped candied ginger, if using, over top. Arrange the bread slices in a single layer over pineapple. Pour custard mixture over bread, and poke bread slices down into custard mixture to make sure they are all moistened. Place baking dish in a larger roasting pan. Place on middle rack in oven. Add enough hot tap water to roasting pan to come halfway up side of baking dish.

Bake pudding in 375-degree oven just until a knife inserted in center comes out clean, about 45 minutes. Remove baking dish from water bath to a wire rack to cool slightly. Serve at cool room temperature or chilled.

I never saw a snow cone until I moved to Ohio with my family when I was fourteen. And there, in Youngstown, at a Friday-night high-school football game, I discovered what was to become a passion in my life, in one form or another: flavored crushed ice. Years later, I learned that what in Ohio is a snow cone, in Italy is called a *granita,* and in France, a *granité.* My favorite snow cone back then was blueberry—I loved having neon-blue lips. That same night I also discovered homemade, thin, very crispy French fries, served in a paper cone and doused with malt vinegar, the way they make and serve them in Belgium and England (something else I didn't know until I began traveling abroad).

As I grew older and discovered another passion in my life, coffee, I combined the two, snow cones and coffee. What I like about this dessert is that it goes with anything, and it's light enough that you can have another dessert with it.

coffee granita

MAKES 6 SERVINGS

3 cups home-brewed very strong coffee
    or espresso
½ to ⅓ cup sugar, to taste

Brew the coffee by your favorite method, and while still hot, stir in the sugar. Let cool. Then refrigerate until thoroughly chilled.

Pour into a metal pie plate, baking pan, or ice-cube trays without dividers. Place in the freezer. When mixture becomes firm and starts to crystallize around the edges, use a fork to break crystals apart and mix lightly into liquid portion. The goal is to evenly distribute the crystals. Return to freezer.

Repeat process two or three more times. When finished, the granita should be evenly firm throughout.

To serve, break into large chunks and spoon into dessert glasses.

serving tips: Spoon a little lightly whipped cream over each, and offer a plate of biscotti, homemade or otherwise.

191

desserts

There's no reason not to have dessert for a weekday supper or a Saturday-night get-together. Fruit crumbles are assembled quickly and use very nonfancy ingredients in the best New England tradition. The key is to select the freshest fruit you can find, whether you're using the peaches called for here, or substituting nectarines, apples, or pears.

peach-and-cranberry crumble with pecans

MAKES 8 SERVINGS

When I was working at The Black Dog restaurant on Martha's Vineyard in the late 1970s and renting a house with friends on the edge of Vineyard Haven, this was the kind of dessert that got quickly gobbled up, whether we made it at home or at the restaurant.

filling

1½ pounds peaches, peeled, pitted, and sliced

1½ cups cranberries, fresh *or* frozen, thawed

⅓ cup packed light-brown sugar

1 tablespoon unsalted butter

1 tablespoon fresh lemon juice

2 teaspoons all-purpose flour

½ teaspoon ground cinnamon

¼ teaspoon ground nutmeg

topping

¾ cup packed light-brown sugar

¾ cup old-fashioned rolled oats

¾ cup all-purpose flour

½ cup (1 stick) unsalted butter, chilled and
    cut into pieces

½ cup pecans, finely chopped

Heat oven to 375 degrees.

filling: In a medium-size bowl, combine the peaches, cranberries, brown sugar, butter, lemon juice, flour, cinnamon, and nutmeg. Spoon mixture into a 10-inch pie plate.

topping: In a medium-size bowl, combine the brown sugar, oats, and flour. Cut in the butter with a pastry blender, or rub mixture with your fingertips until crumbly. Stir in the pecans. Sprinkle over peach-cranberry filling in pie plate.

Bake in 375-degree oven until peaches are tender and topping is golden brown, 40 to 45 minutes. Let stand 15 minutes, then serve.

serving tips: Top with a spoonful of whipped cream, a scoop of vanilla ice cream, or simply a drizzle of heavy cream.

Fruit desserts are some of the easiest to prepare, especially when they rely on fresh, ripe fruit and little else. In practically all cuisines, there is at least one fruit that, with little attention, will satisfy the craving for

fresh pear gratin with cranberries and maple cream

MAKES 8 SERVINGS

something sweet at the end of a meal. The choice can include anything from gooseberries or cherimoya to mangoes or lychee nuts, depending on where you are and the time of year. Since the fruit is the main flavor in this type of dessert, seasonality is important.

Dessert gratins are generally French-inspired, and in this recipe the baking together of the maple syrup and heavy cream creates a creamy, mapley caramel sauce, which nicely blankets the subtly sweet pears and the tart cranberries. The use of a pie plate as the gratin dish exposes a wide surface, encouraging the sauce to reduce and become slightly burnished in spots. This dessert is best served warm.

$\frac{1}{3}$ cup heavy cream

$\frac{1}{4}$ cup maple syrup

1 tablespoon sugar

$\frac{1}{2}$ teaspoon pure vanilla extract

4 firm-ripe pears

$\frac{1}{2}$ cup cranberries, fresh *or* frozen, thawed
  and blotted dry

Heat oven to 350 degrees. In a small bowl, stir together the cream, maple syrup, sugar, and vanilla.

Peel and halve the pears lengthwise, then remove cores with a small spoon or melon baller. With pears, cut side down, on a cutting board, slice each half crosswise into $\frac{1}{4}$-inch-thick slices. Keeping their shape, arrange pear halves in a spoke-pattern in a 10-inch pie plate, with stem ends facing the center. Scatter the cranberries around the pears, and pour the cream mixture over all.

Bake in 350-degree oven until pears are tender, 35 to 45 minutes. Using a spatula, transfer a pear half to each of 8 dessert plates, and spoon a little sauce over each. If pears release a lot of liquid during baking and the sauce is too thin, pour sauce into a pan and gently boil until reduced to the desired consistency. Serve warm.

When it comes to desserts, I have a craving for the rich and creamy, which usually means that heavy cream and/or eggs have to be somewhere in the recipe. The Italians—those creators of all things wonderful—have a category of desserts called *semifreddo,* which simply means "chilled" or "partially frozen." The texture is often like that of a frozen mousse—smooth and not crystalline.

banana *semifreddo* with macadamia nuts

MAKES 8 SERVINGS

About ten years ago, I was overseeing a cookbook project for *Family Circle* magazine that had an impossible schedule of about nine months from start to finish, including the creation of a few hundred new recipes. We were working with a team of very talented recipe developers. One was a professionally trained chef, Sandy Gluck, who has a knack for anything Mediterranean or Italian, and whose husband, Ralph, is also a chef. Talk about home cooking at its best! Their son Nate, who is now about fifteen, was raised on such dishes as sautéed sweet-and-sour bass, smoked salmon, and squid. The semifreddo recipe here is based on one that Sandy created.

When you serve this, you want the *semifreddo* to be just softened enough so a spoon slips easily through without mashing the mixture. For most people who have never tasted one of these frozen concoctions before, the first bite is usually quickly followed by a little "Ooh," and a look of pleasant surprise.

banana *semifreddo* with macadamia nuts

½ cup macadamia nuts
1 pound ripe bananas, peeled and cut
    into chunks
¼ cup packed dark-brown sugar
2 tablespoons dark rum
2 teaspoons fresh lime juice
1 cup heavy cream
1 tablespoon granulated sugar
Pinch salt

Heat oven to 400 degrees. Line an 8½ × 4⅜ × 2¼-inch loaf pan, or a similar-size pan, with plastic wrap, smoothing out the wrinkles as much as possible.

Spread the nuts on a baking sheet. Toast in 400-degree oven until fragrant and lightly golden, 7 to 10 minutes. Transfer to a plate and let cool. Coarsely chop.

In a food processor, combine the bananas, brown sugar, rum, and lime juice. Puree. Scrape into a large bowl. In a small bowl, beat the cream until foamy. Gradually beat in the granulated sugar and salt until soft peaks form. Fold cream mixture into banana mixture. Reserve 2 tablespoons chopped nuts for garnish, and fold remaining nuts into banana mixture. Scrape into lined loaf pan. Cover with plastic wrap. Place in freezer until firm, about 1½ hours or up to 3 days.

To serve, unmold the semifreddo onto a platter. Remove plastic wrap. Let stand at room temperature for 30 minutes or until slightly softened. Slice crosswise, and garnish with reserved nuts.

home cooking

Adriana's Caravan

(good selection of Spanish and Asian ingredients)

321 Grand Central Terminal

New York, NY 10017

Tel: 212-972-8804 or 800-316-0820

Fax: 212-972-8849

www.adrianascaravan.com

ingredient sources

The CMC Company

(very diverse selection of Spanish, Mexican, Thai, Chinese, and Indian ingredients)

P.O. Drawer 322

Avalon, NJ 08202

Tel: 800-262-2780

Fax: 609-861-3065

www.thecmccompany.com

ImportFood

(Thai ingredients, recipes, and starter and gift sets)

P.O. Box 2054

Issaquah, WA 98027

Tel: 425-392-7516

Fax: 425-301-5658

www.importfood.com

Pepperpot

(Indian, Thai, Indonesian, and Malaysian ingredients)

105-123 Carrie Cates Court

Lonsdale Quay Public Market

North Vancouver, British Columbia

Canada V7M 3K7

Tel: 604-986-1877

www.pepperpot.com

Temple of Thai

(Thai ingredients as well as cookbooks, cookware, and recipes)

P.O. Box 112

Carroll, IA 51401

Tel: 712-792-0860 or 877-449-0554

Fax: 712-792-0859

www.templeofthai.com

Alford, Jeffrey, and Naomi Duguid. *Hot Sour Salty Sweet: A Culinary Journey Through Southeast Asia.* Artisan, Workman Publishing, 2000.

Barer-Stein, Thelma, Ph.D. *You Eat What You Are: People, Culture and Food Tradition.* Firefly Books Ltd., 1999.

bibliography

Bladholm, Linda. *The Asian Grocery Store Demystified.* Renaissance Books, 2000.

Brenuil. *Platos Peruanos: Platos Tradicionales Simplificados.* Librerias A.B.C.S.A., 1980.

Certeau, Michel de, Luce Giard, and Pierre Mayol. *The Practice of Everyday Life. Vol. 2: Living and Cooking.* University of Minnesota Press, 1998.

Corn, Charles. *The Scents of Eden: A Narrative of the Spice Trade.* Kodansha International, 1998.

Cost, Bruce. *Asian Ingredients.* Quill, HarperCollins Publishers, 2000.

Davidson, Alan. *The Oxford Companion to Food.* Oxford University Press, 1999.

Fukui, Hayao. *Food and Population in a Northeast Thai Village.* University of Hawaii Press, 1993.

Harris, Jessica B. *The African Cookbook: Tastes of a Continent.* Simon & Schuster, 1998.

Huard, Pierre, and Maurice Durand. *Viet Nam: Civilization and Culture.* Ecole Française d'Extreme-Orient, 1994.

Jue, Joyce. *Williams Sonoma, Savoring Southeast Asia: Recipes and Reflections on Southeast Asian Cooking.* Weldon Owen, Time-Life Books, 2000.

Ly, Van Son. *Vietnamese Cookery Book: 58 Recipes, Delicious Vietnamese Home Cookings.* Dongnai Publishing House, 1995.

Marks, Copeland. *The Exotic Kitchens of Indonesia: Recipes from the Outer Islands.* M. Evans and Company, 1989.

____. *The Exotic Kitchens of Malaysia.* Donald I. Fine Books, 1997.

____. *The Exotic Kitchens of Peru: The Land of the Incas.* M. Evans and Company, 1999.

Marks, Copeland, and Miriam Soeharjo. *The Indonesian Kitchen.* Atheneum, 1981.

Mintz, Sidney W. *Tasting Food, Tasting Freedom: Excursions into Eating, Culture, and the Past.* Beacon Press, 1996.

Mower, Rosalind, ed. *Southeast Asian Specialties: A Culinary Journey Through Singapore, Malaysia and Indonesia.* Culinaria Konemann, 1998.

Ortiz, Elizabeth Lambert. *The Book of Latin American Cooking.* Alfred A. Knopf, 1979.

Owen, Sri. *Indonesian Food and Cookery.* Prospect Books, 1980.

Rojas-Lombardi, Felipe. *The Art of South American Cooking.* HarperCollins Publishers, 1979.

Solomon, Charmaine, with Nina Solomon. *Encyclopedia of Asian Food.* Periplus, 1996.

Trang, Corinne. *Authentic Vietnamese Cooking: Food from a Family Table.* Simon & Schuster, 1999.

Wandee Na Songkhla. *The Royal Favorite Dishes, from the "Hunger Diary" of the Royal Letter No. 42 Written by H. M. Chulachomklao (Rama V) During His European Trip in B.E. 2440.*

No one ever writes a book alone. There are many people who influence what appears on the page, directly and otherwise, and here are the important people who have helped with this journey.

acknowledgments

Dora Jonassen, a friend and professional food stylist, tasted most of the food in this book, and she always had some very cogent suggestions about tinkering with flavor.

Dui Seid, an artist and fellow traveler who opened the door to Asia for me, was another taster who generously shared his insights, gathered from a lifetime of eating in other places.

Tom Reynolds and John Leo have consumed much of my cooking over the years, and their comments always echo in my ears as I stand in front of a stove. Fred Maccarron and Vicky Winter are part of this crew, too.

Susan McQuillan helped with some of the testing, and, as always, listened to my whining. Her three-year-old daughter, Molly, who has a very developed palate, was also part of my taste panel from time to time.

Anki Moromisato showed me Lima, Peru, and taught me about the intricacies of volleyball. Gene Sales shared with me some of his Philippine recipes. Steven Duong of Cyclo restaurant in New York City helped to open doors in Vietnam. Larry LaVigne got me out of the kitchen when it was time for a break.

Manop Charoensuk, Brian Mertens, Bob Halliday, Alex Kerr, and Khajorn Khamkong introduced me to Thailand.

The Tone Brothers of Spice Islands and Durkee seasonings, and Laurel Blair and her staff of Blair Worldwide enhanced my knowledge of Turkey, Indonesia, and India.

Leslie Stoker at Stewart, Tabori & Chang is an editor's editor and an author's dream. The idea for this book was hers. It was to be a casserole book, and together we watched it develop a life of its own, moving in other directions.

Jack Lamplough, director of publicity for Stewart, Tabori & Chang, understood the book from the very beginning.

Barbara Marks is an insightful book designer with whom I've collaborated on many projects. Her willingness to work with an author's jitters about point size and leading at the eleventh hour truly sets her apart as a designer.

Stephen Robert Frankel, a friend and editor, writes more like me than me—a sign of a truly gifted editor.

Liana Fredley, copyeditor and proofreader, focused her skillful eyes on the recipes.

I welcomed the chance to work with Mark Thomas again. His photography, along with Nancy Micklin's propping, and Anne Disrude's food styling (with the help of Maggie Ruggerio), transformed recipes on paper into mouthwatering food portraits. Their cheerful banter made for happy food pictures.

Michael Pederson styled the beautiful cover photo as well as some of the other pictures.

weight equivalents

The metric weights given in this chart are not exact equivalents, but have been rounded up or down slightly to make measuring easier.

conversion charts

avoirdupois	metric
¼ oz	7 g
½ oz	15 g
1 oz	30 g
2 oz	60 g
3 oz	90 g
4 oz	115 g
5 oz	150 g
6 oz	175 g
7 oz	200 g
8 oz (½ lb)	225 g
9 oz	250 g
10 oz	300 g
11 oz	325 g
12 oz	350 g
13 oz	375 g
14 oz	400 g
15 oz	425 g
16 oz (1 lb)	450 g
1½ lb	750 g
2 lb	900 g
2¼ lb	1 kg
3 lb	1.4 kg
4 lb	1.8 kg

volume equivalents

These are not exact equivalents for American cups and spoons, but have been rounded up or down slightly to make measuring easier.

american	metric	imperial
¼ t	1.2 ml	
½ t	2.5 ml	
1 t	5.0 ml	
½ T (1.5 t)	7.5 ml	
1 T (3 t)	15 ml	
¼ cup (4 T)	60 ml	2 fl oz
⅓ cup (5 T)	75 ml	2½ fl oz
½ cup (8 T)	125 ml	4 fl oz
⅔ cup (10 T)	150 ml	5 fl oz
¾ cup (12 T)	175 ml	6 fl oz
1 cup (16 T)	250 ml	8 fl oz
1¼ cups	300 ml	10 fl oz (½ pint)
1½ cups	350 ml	12 fl oz
2 cups (1 pint)	500 ml	16 fl oz
2½ cups	625 ml	20 fl oz (1 pint)
1 quart	1 liter	32 fl oz

oven temperature equivalents

oven mark	f	c	gas
Very cool	250–275	130–140	½–1
Cool	300	150	2
Warm	325	170	3
Moderate	350	180	4
Moderately hot	375	190	5
	400	200	6
Hot	425	220	7
	450	230	8
Very hot	475	250	9

204

205

206

207